Business Research
Reporting

Business Research Reporting

Dorinda Clippinger

BEP BUSINESS EXPERT PRESS

First published in 2018 by
Business Expert Press, LLC
222 East 46th Street, New York, NY 10017
www.businessexpertpress.com

ISBN-13: 978-1-63157-419-1 (paperback)
ISBN-13: 978-1-63157-420-7 (e-book)

Business Expert Press Corporate Communication Collection

Collection ISSN: 2156-8162 (print)
Collection ISSN: 2156-8170 (electronic)

Cover and interior design by S4Carlisle Publishing Services Private Ltd., Chennai, India

First edition: 2018

10 9 8 7 6 5 4 3 2 1

Printed in the United States of America.

Abstract

Business Research Reporting addresses the essential activities of locating, collecting, evaluating, analyzing, interpreting, and reporting of business data. This book is for you if you are

- A business administrator or other professional who must gather original or published data; convert them into objective, organized information; and convey it to others, in or outside your organization.
- An MBA candidate or upper-level student in any professional field in which research is emphasized.

This practical, applied book includes the following useful features:

- Begins each chapter with a case that sets the stage for the discussion that follows.
- Discusses research as a reduction process: raw data reduced to information sets, sets reduced to major findings, and findings reduced to conclusions and recommendations.
- Explains how to know what data are needed and how to evaluate primary and secondary data sources.
- Defines essential terms in two glossaries—one for primary data, one for secondary.
- Identifies data sampling techniques—including both probability and nonprobability designs.
- Describes active and passive data collection methods, including comparisons.
- Explains criteria for primary data collection instruments and explains how to test them for use.
- Describes how to prepare primary data for statistical or nonstatistical data analysis.
- Provides several little-known expedients for web searching. Explores deep-search engines for the invisible web as well as uncommon engines for the visible web.

- Introduces the annotated bibliography as a time-saver in managing secondary sources.
- Offers popular examples of citation management software.
- Models business-friendly APA style for recording and citing secondary sources.
- Demonstrates word-for-word and translated methods of recording secondary data.
- Illustrates how to acknowledge primary and secondary data sources in business reports.

The concise, conversational writing style; bullet points; and many helpful examples and illustrations let you acquire vital information rapidly. Each chapter ends with at least one convenient checklist. In *Business Research Reporting*, you have the basic how-to for reporting research today and in your future!

Keywords

analysis, annotated bibliography, APA, author-date note, citation maker, classification, collection, commercial database, common knowledge, conclusions, copyright infringement, correlation, dark web, deep web, digital library, documentation styles, DOI, dynamic content, fair-use doctrine, field testing, findings, focus group, intellectual property, measurement scales, meta-search engines, microforms, parametric, paraphrased, plagiarism checker, primary data, probability, proprietary database, public domain, recommendations, refereed journal, references, reliability, sampling, secondary data, standard curve, validity, variance, verbatim, visible web

Contents

Preface

Business Research Reporting aims to help business managers, MBA candidates, and upper-level college students boost their research skills and report their research with confidence. This book highlights the value of research to making business decisions and solving business problems—and does so in a clear, commonsense way. For example, the author advises readers facing a business problem to begin with secondary research and then to proceed with primary research only if the published data do not lead to a workable solution.

In the book's four chapters, readers obtain practical answers to their questions and concerns about conducting research and reporting the results orally and in writing. Content is arranged as follows:

- Chapter 1 introduces business research; specifically, collecting primary data. It provides a basis for evaluating primary data sources and explains the sampling concept. In addition, the chapter explores probability and nonprobability sampling designs and tells the circumstances for using each design. Basic concepts of measurement and scales are presented as background for preparing data-gathering instruments.

- Chapter 2 uses scenarios from the first chapter to explore data analysis. It offers advice for editing and coding data before analyzing it. The chapter also emphasizes the importance of reviewing the business problem and research purpose frequently as data are collected and analyzed. Various statistical and nonstatistical means for analyzing both qualitative and quantitative data are explored. The three levels of data interpretation—findings, conclusions, and recommendations—are delineated and illustrated.

- Chapter 3 shows business researchers how to locate, evaluate, and extract data from various web sources and brick-and-mortar libraries. Specifically, the chapter gives pointers for using a style guide and an annotated bibliography of useful sources. Optimized search techniques are discussed, along with deep-web and social-media search engines that provide maximum efficiency. The chapter also offers data evaluation criteria and recommendations for simplifying data recording.

- Chapter 4 explains and illustrates how to acknowledge data sources in written and oral research reports. In addition, it explores the critical issues of copyright infringement and plagiarism, including guides for avoiding both. The chapter demonstrates how to produce a references list, giving many up-to-date examples of various digital and print sources and how to cite sources in your writing and speaking. Information about using free, online reference management software is included.

Business Research Reporting can be your go-to guidebook for years to come. Reading through it in a couple of hours, you can pick up ample information that you can apply instantly. Then keep this book handy and refer to it as the need arises in your research reporting activities.

Please contact the author with your suggestions for improving future editions of *Business Research Reporting*.

Acknowledgments

Thank you, Dr. Shirley Kuiper, for laying the groundwork for this book some years ago. I'm also grateful to you, Dr. Debbie DuFrene, for turning rough copy into these enlightening chapters. I appreciate you, too, William Jewell, for unwavering support on the home front. And I'm grateful to many business associates and students for influencing my thinking about communication and education for business over the years.

CHAPTER 1

Gathering Primary Research Data

Alan R. Belcher, PhD
Ashford University

Welcome to the world of business research. You may be reading this book to find out how to do research methodically; you may be reading to find out how to solve problems; you may be reading just to find out what "research" is all about. This book will provide the basics of the research process and will give you a strong starting point on building your own research projects. This chapter covers a wide range of things to consider as you get started. Some readers will already know much of this, while others are just getting started. In either case, you will find information about the terms and processes involved in research.

Business people are continuously solving problems. You have likely identified one or more business problems or opportunities that you think require some research to reach the right answer. You may ask yourself, what is involved in research? Generally, there are three steps to any research project.

1. You have to ask the right question.
2. You gather data.
3. You analyze the data and make sense of it.

Once you have defined the problem or opportunity, Step 1 may be done, although there is possibly more to do with defining the problem.

Undoubtedly, you need to define an actual Problem, not just symptoms of a problem. Defining a research problem will *become clearer as we go through this chapter.*

We will talk about data collection. Collecting data can be easy or complicated, depending on the approach you take. Making it easy requires us to know about different types of data, ways to acquire data, and how to ensure that the data accurately answer the questions we have asked.

When we talk about different types of data, one major distinction separates primary data and secondary data. *Primary data* is data that you generate yourself. *Secondary data* is data that someone has collected previously and you are reviewing it for your own purpose.

A second way of distinguishing data is by the terms of quantitative and qualitative. *Quantitative data* is typically represented by a set of numbers while *qualitative data* is represented in words, ideas, and thoughts. We will consider these different types of data as we work through examples of data collection.

Case 1.1
A Business Research Scenario

Assume you own a small, independent grocery store. You sell typical groceries: dairy, meat, produce, deli, canned goods, baking items, cleaning products, paper goods, pet food, sodas, beer, wine, and other products. Most of your customers are regulars in the store, and you pride yourself on knowing them individually, many by name. Your customers are of all types; your community is fairly diverse in age, income, and ethnicity. One of the things you believe you need to do is to be more proactive in stocking shelves with products your customers want. Of course, one of your biggest concerns is inventory.

From time to time you think to yourself: It would be nice to know what goods and services my customers think they are going to want or need in the next few months or year. That is your basic research question. The work now is for you to go about finding out from your customers what their anticipated needs are. If you only had a handful of customers, you could call them and ask the questions directly; but you have too many customers for that. In fact, you have several hundred customers who rely on you on a regular basis for groceries, so how are you Going to find out what those people are thinking? You also have several occasional shoppers, and you know you want to expand your customer base as well.

Basically, you are hoping to do a few things to improve your operation of the grocery store. You want to:

- Anticipate seasonal buying trends.
- Determine what opportunities you are missing.
- Compare your store to other markets.
- Find out if your customers are satisfied with service, cleanliness of the store, and so on.

Case 1.1 will be our example as we continue this discussion of gathering primary data. Feel free to substitute your own business venture as appropriate.

You are probably already thinking about ways you can ask and find answers to these questions, and that constitutes research. We will discuss the research tools that will help to ensure that your effort in research provides quality results.

Evaluating Primary Data Sources

As noted, when we collect data through our own efforts, not just reviewing data that were previously collected, we call that primary data. There are a number of factors to consider when collecting primary data:

- Qualities of data: validity, reliability, and practicality
- Sampling issues: accuracy and precision
- Strategies for sampling: probability and non-probability
- Instruments for gathering data easily and consistently

When we collect data, there are some aspects of that data that we must consider. Above all, we want to be sure that the effort, time, and expense that we put into data collection are worthwhile. The qualities of data that we will consider are validity, reliability, and practicality.

Validity

Validity is a measurement concept that refers to the extent to which differences revealed with a measuring tool represent true differences among the people or objects being measured. In a broader sense, validity can apply to primary data sources and the data obtained from those sources, as well as to the instruments used to collect data.

A data source is valid if it is able to provide objective, accurate information about the research topic. Some sources have greater degrees of validity than others. For example, assume your research requires information about the number of single-parent households in your county. The 2010 U.S. census (secondary source) has greater validity than would a heads-of-household sample in the county conducted by your staff (primary source) because the data come from a more extensive survey than you could conduct yourself. In contrast, assume your research requires data about average cost-of-living pay increases granted in your county last year. In that case, a survey of local businesses could be more valid than the census data because it is more current and specific.

For collected data to be considered valid, those data must actually answer the research question. If we think for a moment about a politician and how that politician might respond to a question, we know that, many times, the answer is really a non-answer. From a research statistical point of view, that answer would not be considered valid. In order to collect valid data in your research project, you will want to ensure that you are asking good and logical questions and that the possible answers you will receive will help you answer the research questions.

Let's assume that one of the questions you want to ask of your customers is their household income. If you construct the question with an open-ended response possibility, customers could answer with an exact amount or with a vague descriptor of their income. To help ensure valid responses, you will probably want to create a question that forces specific answers as shown in the following example.

What is your annual household income? (Check one)

- Less than $20,000
- $20,001 to $40,000
- $40,001 to $60,000
- More than $60,000

How many are in your household? (Check one)

- More than 5
- 4 to 5
- 2 to 3
- 1
- Prefer not to answer

In this way, your customers must respond to the question by selecting one of these categories. Not only will this type of question reduce the possibilities of a wide range of answers, it will also help to ensure that you are getting the kinds of answers you need to answer your questions: valid answers. However, it is also helpful to provide opportunity for customers to opt out of responding to a question if they simply prefer not to answer any question that may be sensitive in nature to them.

Reliability

Reliability is a measure of repeatability. Data are considered reliable when a repeat of the questions to the same audience will produce the same or nearly the same responses. Reliability is important because you want to be sure the answers you receive are not merely random or chance. It means that if you surveyed a different random subset of the same audience, you would get similar results. Now, in the case of the sample question about household income, we know that household income may change over time and that's to be expected. However, we want to be sure that the answers are consistent over time in terms of how accurate the responses are based on the questions we asked.

Reliability is also a measurement concept that refers to the consistency of results obtained with a measuring device. A reliable data collection instrument is relatively free of random or unstable error; such an instrument helps the researcher get as close to the truth as possible. For example, a steel measuring rod is more reliable than a cloth measuring tape to measure distance or height. The steel rod itself changes little with variations in temperature, moisture, or pressure; but a cloth measuring tape may stretch or shrink in response to those conditions.

Two aspects of consistency, stability and equivalence, contribute to reliability. An instrument has *stability* if it gives consistent measurements of the same person or thing at different times; for example, your car odometer records nearly the same mileage each time you measure the distance of the route from your home to your workplace. The instrument has *equivalence* if different people using the instrument at approximately the same time and for the same purpose get consistent results; both you and your spouse or a friend get the same results when measuring distance by the odometer.

The concept of reliability extends to primary data sources, and data obtained from them, as well as to data collection instruments. In your grocery store, you may want to identify services that will attract more customers. A sample of individuals in a specific income range within the geographic area you plan to serve would be a more reliable data source than would your current customers. Your current customers' perceptions are not necessarily representative of people who do not shop at your store.

Ideally, data sources and data collection techniques are both reliable and valid. Valid instruments and sources are also reliable, but reliable sources or instruments are not necessarily valid. Assume, for example, that survey participants mistakenly believe they have used a toothpaste (Product X) that is similar to but different from the toothpaste they have actually used (Product Y). The participants may consistently report satisfaction with Product X (reliability), but the information is not valid because they have never used that product. They are clearly reporting satisfaction with something but not with the test toothpaste.

Here is another example to illustrate the relationship between validity and reliability. Automobile odometers, which measure travel distance and speed, are calibrated to be used with certain tire sizes. If an auto owner installs a tire larger in diameter than that for which the odometer was calibrated, the odometer will consistently (reliably) register a speed that is lower than the auto is actually traveling. By using a reliable instrument that records incorrect (invalid) data, the driver may have an unpleasant experience with the highway patrol.

As you select primary data sources, always consider both the validity and the reliability of each source.

Practicality

A final criterion by which you must judge potential primary data sources is practicality. Although business researchers desire validity and reliability, some tradeoffs are usually needed between the ideal project and what can be achieved within time and budget constraints.

Practicality refers to both the cost and the convenience of using a data source. Assume, for example, that you want to investigate customer satisfaction with your products and customer service. Your store's customers are certainly a more valid data source than are your employees. Observation of customers interacting with employees and face-to-face interviews with customers may be your preferred data-gathering techniques. The time and cost required to use those techniques, however, may force you to substitute a less expensive survey technique, such as a preaddressed questionnaire given to customers with their purchases. As you prepare your questionnaire, you may believe that increasing the number of items is one way to improve questionnaire reliability. However, since survey participants often resist completing a long questionnaire, you may shorten the questionnaire, thereby trading a degree of reliability for practicality.

If you want to try to determine the likelihood of your customers' willingness to continue being customers even with a 2% price increase, you could ask every customer that question. But, is it practical to ask every customer every question on your survey? Let's think about a slightly different example. If we wanted to know for whom everyone in a particular state was going to vote for governor, we could call and ask every voter in the state. But again, that is not really practical. What is more practical is to ask the questions of a subset of the voters. Likewise, for your customers, it is more practical to ask a subset or a sample of the entire population of your customers. This brings us to define two important words when thinking about business research: population and sample.

Sampling Primary Data Sources

To understand sampling concepts, you must understand five terms: population, element, sample, subject, and population frame.

Population refers to the entire group of people, events, or other items of interest that are the focus of a study. If you want to know customers' opinions about the store's products and services, the population is all members of the community who do or might shop at your store. An *element* is a single unit of the population, that is, one individual of the community. The population, therefore, consists of the total collection of elements about which a researcher wishes to make inferences. A *sample* is a subgroup of the population composed of some of the elements, and a *subject* is a single member of the sample.

Before a sample can be drawn from a population, all members of the population must be identified. A *population frame* (sometimes called a sampling frame) is a list of all elements in a population from which a sample could be drawn. In some cases, devising that list is relatively easy; for example, an accurate list of current customers should be relatively easy to identify. But, in the case where you wish to identify all members of the community as the population, that may be nearly impossible; and a list that reasonably approximates the population must be used. For example, if you wanted to know what the community thought of your grocery store, identifying all members of the community would be prohibitive. Some researchers use a telephone directory as the population frame when they wish to sample a city population. However, with the current popularity of cell phones, many city residents have no land-based telephones; and others have unlisted numbers. Therefore, the telephone directory is not a true representation of the population. To obtain valid data, you would do well to avoid using that source as its population frame. A list of registered voters in the areas served might be a better population frame for your grocery store research.

In business research, an investigation may involve hundreds or thousands of potential subjects. Time and budget constraints often prohibit data collection from or about every element that could be studied; therefore, a sample is used. The basic idea of sampling is that elements in a population provide useful data about the characteristics of that population.

When you judge the quality of a box of chocolate truffles, for example, you take a sample (one truffle), analyze the characteristics of that sample, and generalize that the entire population (all truffles in the box) has the same characteristics. Similarly, in your grocery store's customer satisfaction survey, you infer that the characteristics of a sample of those customers represent the characteristics of the entire customer population. Such inferences, however, are valid only if the sample is valid.

For a research project, the population is everyone about whom you wish to draw conclusions. In our grocery store example, the population could be defined as all your current customers, or possibly, all potential customers. We know that it is not likely that your survey or collection of data will touch all current or potential customers. So, we must choose a sample, or subset, of people from your customer database.

Characteristics of a Valid Sample

Sampling is the process of selecting a subset of records to review or a subset of individuals to survey. When you consider the population of all customers, you know it is not very practical to think that you will be able to survey or receive some data from all customers. So, you will take a sample. Of course, the larger the sample compared to the population, the more likely that the sample is representative of the entire population. There are a few considerations you will need to make about your sampling to be sure that the data you collect and prepare to analyze will be valuable.

A *valid sample* is one that accurately represents its population characteristics. Sample validity depends on three factors: accuracy, precision, and size.[1]

Accuracy

An accurate sample is free of *bias*; that is, it neither overrepresents nor underrepresents certain population characteristics. An accurate sample has no *systematic variance*, which is variation in measurement due to some known or unknown influence that causes the scores to lean in a particular direction. For example, assume that a group of young professionals meets for coffee at your store's café every Tuesday from 7 to 8 a.m. If the store draws a sample from members who visit during those hours, the sample may be systematically biased toward the attitudes of young professionals. The attitudes of retired members who use your store primarily during other hours of the day would be systematically underrepresented.

Precision

No sample can be identical to its population in all respects. A *sample statistic* (such as the arithmetic mean of the sample) may be expected to vary from its corresponding population value (the arithmetic mean of the population) because of random fluctuations in the sampling process. Such fluctuations or variations are referred to as *sampling error*. A precise sample has little sampling error.

Assume, for example, that you want information about customers who are retired. For practical reasons, you may decide to take a sample of customers who come to the store between 11:30 a.m. and 1 p.m. because that is when retirees tend to shop. But a sample taken at that time would contain sampling error if it randomly included guests who accompanied members to the store for lunch that day or young professionals who were stopping by at that time to pick up something for the office.

Sample Size

Precision and accuracy are important sampling issues because a researcher wants to be sure that inferences about the population are justifiable. Sample size can affect the accuracy and precision of your inferences.

Generally, if the characteristics that are being studied are widely dispersed in the population, the accuracy and precision of inferences based on the sample can be improved by increasing the sample size. For example, if the monthly expenditures of your store's retired members range from $50 to $300, to gain the desired levels of precision and accuracy, the researcher will have to draw a larger sample than would be necessary if the monthly expenditures were $5 to $30. In contrast, if the characteristics are narrowly dispersed in the population, drawing a large sample size may be wasteful and costly. It may be possible to achieve the desired precision and accuracy with a relatively small sample. By following the guides given in the next section, you should be able to select an appropriate sample size for your research.

Guides for Determining Sample Size

Three rules of thumb guide researchers in determining sample size.

- Sample sizes larger than 30 and smaller than 500 are appropriate for most research. Where samples are to be broken into subsamples (such as males and females or juniors and seniors), a minimum sample size of 30 for each category is necessary.
- If several variables are used in the research, the sample size should be several times (preferably 10 times or more) as large as the number of variables measured in the study. For example, if you are measuring four variables, your sample size should be at least 40.
- For simple experimental research with tight experimental controls, successful research is possible with samples as small as 10 or 20.

A final consideration in sampling is the kind of sample to use. Several options are available. The nature of your research problem and the desired degree of accuracy determine which sampling technique is appropriate.

Sampling Designs

Sampling designs fall into two major categories: probability and nonprobability. In *probability sampling*, the population elements have a known chance or probability of being selected. In *nonprobability sampling*, the elements do not have a predetermined chance of being selected.

Probability Sampling

When representativeness of the sample is important, probability sampling is used. This type of sampling can be unrestricted or restricted.

Unrestricted probability sampling is commonly called simple random sampling. *Restricted or complex sampling* designs have been developed to compensate for the inefficiencies of unrestricted sampling. Four of those designs—systematic, stratified random, cluster, and area sampling—are used frequently in business research.

Simple Random Sampling

In *simple random sampling*, every element in the population has an equal chance of being selected as a subject. Assume that your grocery store has 1,000 regular customers and wishes to draw a sample of 100. If all names are thrown into a basket and a blindfolded individual draws 100, each member has an equal chance (100 in 1,000, or 1 in 10) of being drawn.

Simple random sampling has the least bias, but the technique can be cumbersome and expensive. In addition, bias can enter the sample if the population frame is not accurate and up to date.

Restricted or Complex Sampling

The *systematic sampling* design involves drawing every nth element in the population, starting with a randomly chosen element. To draw a systematic sample of 100, you would randomly select a member number, such as 128, and then draw every tenth (if that is the chosen n) account thereafter (138, 148, 158, and so on) until 100 have been drawn.

Accuracy of this method depends on an accurate population frame. In addition, researchers using this technique must be cautious to avoid systematic bias. For example, a researcher may decide to draw a systematic sample of 25 companies from the most recent list of the Fortune 500 largest industries, drawing every tenth firm after randomly selecting a starting point. Assume the starting number is 201. Although the population frame may be up to date, this design would systematically bias the sample toward the smallest firms. Number 1 on the list is the largest firm, but the sample would be drawn from numbers 201 through 441. This problem could be avoided by using a larger interval (such as 20) that would require returning to the beginning of the list after the number 500 was reached. This example illustrates that a researcher must be aware of the characteristics of the population frame before defining the *n* to use in systematic sampling.

Stratified Random Sampling

The *stratified random sampling* design requires stratification or segregation of the elements, followed by a random selection of subjects from the strata. To draw this type of sample, the grocery store could stratify its members by age-groups corresponding approximately to education and career stages, such as 21 to 30, 31 to 40, 41 to 50, 51 to 60, and over 60. Then the store would determine what kind of sample it requires from each age group to achieve the objectives of the study.

For *proportionate sampling*, the store would draw a number from each stratum that is proportionate to the percentage of the total population represented by elements in that stratum. Figure 1.1 shows the number of subjects to be drawn from each stratum if the grocery store wishes to draw a proportionate stratified random sample of 100 from its 1,000 members.

For *disproportionate sampling*, elements are drawn from each stratum based on the researcher's judgment. One factor that justifies disproportionate sampling is extreme imbalance in strata sizes warranting more or less than proportional representation of certain strata. That situation exists in the proportionate sample shown in Figure 1.1. The disproportionate sample in that table shows how a researcher could adjust a sample

Population Strata	N	Percent	Proportionate (N = 200)	Disproportionate (N = 200)
21–30	200	20	40	40
31–40	250	25	50	47
41–50	300	30	60	50
51–60	190	19	38	38
Over 60	60	6	12	25
Total	1,000	100	200	200

Figure 1.1 Proportionate and disproportionate stratified random samples

to compensate for small numbers in certain categories. Disproportionate sampling is also used at times because it is convenient, simple, and economical to administer.

Cluster Sampling

A *cluster sampling* technique may be appropriate when a targeted population is already divided into groups or can easily be clustered. After defining the clusters, the researcher randomly selects some of those clusters and studies all elements in each cluster. Ideally, the clusters demonstrate heterogeneity (diversity) within and homogeneity (similarity) across groups. In the grocery store case, for example, ideal clusters would contain many different kinds of members (that is, varied by age, gender, profession, years of being a customer, and so forth) but all clusters would represent the "typical" club member, whatever the research has determined is "typical."

Naturally occurring clusters, such as clusters of students or residents, are often used in business research. But those clusters typically are relatively homogeneous within and heterogeneous *across* groups. For example, home owners clustered by neighborhoods tend to be similar within groups but different across groups. For that reason, naturally occurring clusters, although convenient for some kinds of research, tend to lack the precision and accuracy desired in samples.

Area Sampling

When research can be identified with some geographic region, area sampling is appropriate. *Area sampling* is a form of cluster sampling in which a sample is drawn from a defined geographic area.

This technique is efficient and relatively inexpensive. Suppose, for example, that you want to survey the residents of the northeast section of the city to determine the feasibility of opening a store in that area. Obtaining a complete list of all adults in that area would be potentially difficult. But it would be relatively easy to look at a map, define the area commonly considered the "northeast section," and draw a sample of homes by street addresses.

Nonprobability Sampling

Nonprobability sampling is appropriate when a researcher's objective is to gather preliminary information in a quick and inexpensive way rather than to make generalizations about a larger population. There are also times when nonprobability sampling is the only feasible technique. For example, probability sampling could not be used for an analysis of the content of internal reports because it would be impossible to construct the population frame of all internal reports. Some reports would be too confidential to release for research purposes, some would have been misplaced or destroyed, and some, such as oral reports, would not have been recorded in a permanent form. Nonprobability sampling takes two forms: convenience and purposive.

Convenience Sampling

A *convenience sample* is unrestricted; the researcher is free to choose elements according to their availability. This technique is easy and relatively inexpensive, and it satisfies the demands of some research designs.

Assume, for example, that you want some preliminary information about additional goods or services in which customers might be interested. Your store might draw a convenience sample by placing a set of questionnaires at the door of the store with a sign saying "Tell us how we can serve you." Although the sample could not possibly represent the total customer population, the results of the survey would provide worthwhile clues about customer interests. Similarly, interviewing a convenience sample of people as they leave the opening performance in a new concert hall could provide valuable information to the hall manager about the positive and negative aspects of the building (acoustics, seats, restrooms, and so on) and identify needed adjustments.

Purposive Sampling

A *purposive sample* is a nonprobability sample that conforms to certain criteria. There are two major types: judgment and quota sampling.

In a *judgment* sample, the researcher handpicks elements that conform to certain criteria. This technique is used when only limited numbers of people possess the information that is sought or when elements are chosen because of their predictive power in the past. For example, if you want to investigate what it takes for a woman to become a partner in a Wall Street law firm, you might appropriately seek information only from women who have achieved that status. Political analysts use judgment sampling when they predict the outcome of an election by projecting from results of a few precincts whose voting records in the past have predicted election results.

In a *quota sample*, the researcher tries to ensure that the sample is representative of the population from which it is drawn by specifying certain control dimensions. The dimensions selected must have a known distribution in the population, and they must be relevant to the topic studied.

Assume, for example, that you wish to conduct a study at your state's flagship university to determine student opinion about required drug testing for student athletes. You may hypothesize that differences in attitudes may be related to gender, athletics team membership, and class level. You could assume two categories for each dimension and determine what percent of the student population fits into each category as shown in this example.

Gender	Female	57%
	Male	43%
Athletics Team	Member	29%
	Nonmember	71%
Class Level	Undergraduate	87%
	Graduate	13%

You would then draw a convenience sample, choosing subjects until you have secured the same proportions of males and females, athletics team members and nonmembers, and undergraduate and graduate students that make up the student population.

An obvious weakness of quota sampling is that the sample may not be representative of the population; hence, the researcher's ability to generalize (draw conclusions) from the findings is limited. For example, you could conceivably draw your entire quota from students enrolled in the humanities, whose opinions might differ widely from those of students enrolled in business or engineering. Researchers can protect the sample from such bias, however, by careful selection of relevant dimensions that define the quota. In this example, including the course of study as a dimension would have forced you to avoid selecting all subjects from one academic area.

A special nonprobability method using a referral sample, or *snowball sample*, can be useful when the desired sample attribute is extremely hard to find. Snowball sampling relies on referrals from initial subjects to generate additional ones. For instance, a manufacturer of knitting kits is considering changing the product's image and redesigning its packaging to appeal to men and women aged 18 to 34. Not surprisingly, the manufacturer has difficulty finding people in that age group who knit. Therefore, when the company's research associates identify a few subjects, they ask those respondents to refer to them other knitters they know. This useful sampling technique does introduce bias because it decreases the likelihood that the sample will truly represent the population. At the same time, referral sampling can lower research costs when subjects are scarce.

Preparing Instruments to Collect Primary Data

Primary data collection tools consist of observation forms, questionnaires, and interview guides. To design those tools, you must understand some basic concepts about measurement and measurement scales.

Measurement and Measurement Scales

Measurement is the process of assigning numbers to an element or characteristic that is being observed or analyzed, and a *measurement scale* is any device used to assign numbers to the characteristic. Height—the distance from the bottom to the top of something standing upright—is a common measurement with which you are familiar. Height can be scaled in inches, feet, yards, centimeters, millimeters, or meters.

A primary purpose of measurement is to permit analysis and comparisons of relevant characteristics. For example, through measurement of an infant's height at birth and at age 3 months, you can learn something about the child's growth. By comparing those measurements with the average measurements for children in your culture, you obtain additional information about the child's growth rate.

In business research, you will frequently want to measure and compare behavior, attitudes, desires, or other characteristics of a target group of people. Four scales are commonly used to measure or assign numbers to such data: nominal, ordinal, interval, and ratio.

Nominal

A *nominal scale* allows you to classify information and assign a number to each classification. The classifications used for nominal scales must be all-inclusive and mutually exclusive. For example, every survey respondent can be classified with respect to age if the group identifiers are defined correctly (for example, under 50 or 50 and older). In a customer survey, your store may wish to categorize respondents by type of products purchased:

1. Fresh produce
2. Meat and dairy
3. Non-perishable foods
4. Paper goods

A nominal scale merely permits assignment of numbers to the categories that are of interest to the researcher. Consequently, the statistics that can be computed from a nominal scale are limited to such descriptive items as the percentage of responses in each category and the mode—that is, which category has the greatest number of responses. A nominal scale provides no information about relative value of the items classified. A number does not indicate that items in any category are better or worse or weaker or stronger than items in another category.

Ordinal

An *ordinal scale* permits determination of a qualitative difference among categories. Assume the grocery store manager wants to know which proposed new services are most attractive to consumers. Respondents could be asked to indicate their preferences by ranking five services as shown in the following example. Assume that the numbers in the "rank" column are one subject's responses, with 1 representing the most preferred and 5 the least preferred service.

Service	Rank
1. Online shopping	2
2. "Quick Lunch" menu/service, Monday–Friday	4
3. Wireless Internet service	3
4. Senior discount (half-price)	5
5. Home delivery	1

An ordinal scale helps the researcher determine the percentage of respondents who consider half-price "Senior discount" most important, the percentage who consider a "Quick Lunch" most important, and so on. Such a scale also shows that the individual who ranked the services as shown prefers "Senior discount" to all other services. The respondent also prefers a "Quick Lunch" menu and wireless Internet service to home delivery or online shopping. But the ranking does not indicate the relative strength of the preferences. The individual may consider the first-ranked item to be only slightly more important than the second-ranked item, but the respondent may think that the item given the second rank is considerably more important than the third-ranked service.

Interval

If the store wants to analyze the strength of differences in attitudes toward various services, you must use an *interval scale*. Such a scale presents equally spaced (or equal-appearing) points on a continuum to represent order, differences, and magnitude of differences. Although five-point interval scales are common, any number of points may be used. On the basis of the research problem, the researcher must decide how refined the measure should be.

The following example illustrates how the club might use an interval scale to determine the strength of preferences for various services.

Indicate how important each of the following services is to you by circling the number on the scale that reflects your attitude:

1 = Very unimportant
2 = Unimportant
3 = Neutral
4 = Important
5 = Extremely important

Service	Rating				
1. Online shopping	1	2	3	4	5
2. "Quick Lunch" menu/service, Monday–Friday	1	2	3	4	5
3. Wireless Internet service	1	2	3	4	5
4. Senior discount	1	2	3	4	5
5. Home delivery	1	2	3	4	5

An interval scale permits calculation of an arithmetic mean for each variable. Such a scale also permits calculation of the variance and standard deviation to analyze how responses are distributed around the mean.

An interval scale begins at an arbitrary point other than zero. The scale in the foregoing illustration begins at 1, but it could have started with any number. Since the scale does not begin at zero, it cannot measure the proportions of differences. Although the distances between points on the scale are assumed to be equal, a value of 5 cannot be interpreted as five times greater than a value of 1. Considering a Fahrenheit thermometer will help you understand that characteristic of an interval scale. A thermometer's scale range may be from a point below zero, −50 degrees for example, to a point above zero, such as +150 degrees. After using the thermometer to record outdoor temperature every day at noon for a month, you can compute the average noontime temperature for that month. But if the temperature is 80 degrees at noon one day and 60 the next day, you cannot say that the temperature has fallen by 25 percent; you can only say that it has fallen by 20 degrees.

Ratio

A *ratio scale* has an absolute zero point and equal intervals on the scale, making it the most powerful measurement scale. Some examples of ratio scales are income, age, height, and weight. This scale permits calculation of the magnitude of differences. For example, a $20,000 income is one-third of a $60,000 income, a 75-year-old person has lived three times longer than a 25-year-old person, a 90-foot structure is 50 percent taller than a 60-foot structure, and an object that weighs 260 pounds is twice as heavy as an object weighing 130 pounds.

Although the ratio scale is the most powerful scale, it cannot be used for some kinds of measurement. When measuring a behavioral characteristic, such as attitude, it is rarely logical to assume that an individual completely lacks the characteristic that is being studied. For example, most store patrons have some attitude or opinion about the desirability of various services, even if the attitude is that a particular service is very unimportant. Logic requires, therefore, that scales used to measure most behavioral dimensions begin at a point above zero.

The type of measurement scale—nominal, ordinal, interval, or ratio—determines what kinds of statistics can be used for data analysis. Any statistic that can be computed from less powerfully scaled data (that is, nominal or ordinal) can be computed on more powerfully scaled data (that is, interval and ratio). But many statistics that can be computed for interval or ratio data cannot be applied to nominal or ordinal data.

To design an effective instrument for primary data collection, you must first decide which measurement scale or scales will help you collect and analyze the data needed to solve your research problem. After making that decision, you must design the instrument carefully and test it before beginning your actual collection. In addition, in some research, such as in questionnaire surveys, you must also prepare a transmittal message to stimulate potential respondents to participate in the study.

Criteria for Instrument Design

All primary data collection instruments must meet certain design standards. The overall objective is that the instrument must enable someone (the observer, interviewer, or subject) to record valid data in a manner that permits analysis. To achieve that objective, the tool must meet criteria related to content, language, format, and instructions. As you read the following criteria, notice their application in Figures 1.2 through 1.5.

Content

The content of the data collection instrument must be justified in terms of its relevance to the research problem. Research time and money are wasted if irrelevant items are included. To determine relevance, ask yourself what purpose each item serves, using this checklist.

❑ *Is the question required to establish rapport or to screen potential subjects?* Even though specific answers to such a question may not be part of the data analysis, the question may be relevant because it facilitates the data collection process. For example, the question "Approximately how long have you been shopping at this store?" can establish rapport by providing an opening, nonthreatening question that stimulates conversation. That question can also be a screening device. If you wish to interview members who have patronized the store for more than 2 years, the answer indicates whether to continue or discontinue the interview.

❑ *Is the information required for the data analysis plan?* Demographic data, such as gender or age of participant, may be relevant if data analysis calls for comparisons by gender or age. But if such comparisons are not planned, questions about gender or age should not be included.

❑ *Is this the best way to obtain the information?* If the information can be obtained in another way, the time of observers or respondents should not be wasted. For example, if store records show the date a customer first shopped there, that information should not be sought unless it is used to establish rapport or to screen participants on the basis of length of membership.

❑ *Is this question (or observation) capable of generating valid data?* If a question is offensive or unduly taxes a respondent's memory, the person may refuse to answer or may fabricate an answer. If a question is biased or leading, the respondent may unknowingly provide invalid data. In some situations, subjects will provide answers they think are acceptable rather than admit lack of knowledge or understanding. An observer may also record inaccurate or fictitious data if the observation form demands more than the observer can handle capably.

Language

The overall effect of the language should be to encourage people to participate and provide accurate information. To achieve that effect, the language used in instructions and questions must be positive and confident (but not condescending), clear, unbiased, and neutral (not leading). The following examples illustrate the effects of language.

Condescending

You may not know it, but the state legislature is debating whether to reduce the number of weeks that an unemployed person may be eligible for unemployment benefits.

Positive, Confident

The state legislature is debating whether to reduce the number of weeks that an unemployed person may be eligible for unemployment benefits. The primary issue is that the recent high rate of unemployment has nearly depleted the unemployment insurance fund and is requiring the state to increase the unemployment taxes imposed on employers. What are your attitudes toward decreasing the number of weeks that an umemployed person may be eligible for unemployment benefits?

Presumptuous

I'm sure you will agree that we all have an obligation to help unemployed individuals meet their basic needs. That's why I'm conducting this study.

Encouraging, Confident

You can help improve the state's unemployment compensation program. Your answers, along with those of others, will help to identify critical unemployment issues for our legislators to consider during the coming legislative session.

Unclear, Leading

What do you think the Chamber of Commerce should do to reduce the negative impact of cruise ships in Charleston Harbor? (Assumes that respondent knows all options that the Chamber can pursue; assumes that respondent opposes the presence of cruise ships in the local harbor.) *Clear:* Which of the following actions would you support to improve relationships between local residents and cruise passengers? (Follow the question with a list of actions the Chamber is considering.)

Biased

Do you support public financing for all federal elections to take back control from the special interests? (Tends to lead toward "yes" because of negative connotation of "special interests.")

Unbiased

Do you support public financing for all federal elections?

Leading

Do you think there should be more public funding of the arts and arts education since private support of the arts has declined by more than 50 percent during the last 10 years? (A "no" to this question could suggest that the respondent lacks an appreciation for the arts.)

Neutral

Under what conditions should the state legislature continue to fund arts education in elementary and secondary schools?

Format

The format of observation forms, interview guides, and questionnaires must contribute to readability, ease of completion, and accuracy. In addition, questionnaire format should entice subjects to complete the questionnaire rather than discourage them from doing so. The following guides will help you achieve those objectives.

- Provide enough space to record information neatly and clearly. If insufficient space is provided, respondents may become discouraged and decide not to provide all data, or they may enter the information illegibly.
- Use blank space advantageously. All margins should be at least one inch, and sufficient space should be placed between items to avoid a crowded, oppressive appearance.
- Place spaces or boxes for responses near the items to be answered. This practice contributes to accuracy. If the answer spaces are too far from the items, the respondent may accidentally use the wrong space or select an unintended answer.
- Choose open and closed question formats wisely. Open items state a question or make a statement to be completed by the respondent. No answer options are provided. Open items are appropriate when the researcher wants to probe for a range of responses or when the range is known to be so broad that it is impossible to list all options. Because the answers can vary considerably, responses to open items are difficult to process. Open items also lead into qualitative data which requires an intensive review of comments in order to find themes and draw conclusions.
- Closed items provide a list of anticipated answers from which the respondent chooses. Closed items are appropriate when the range of responses can be anticipated or when the researcher wants to force responses into ranges that have been defined in the research problem. Options for closed items must be all-inclusive and mutually exclusive (do not overlap); that is, all possible answers must be included, and concepts or categories contained

in the options must not overlap. The following example illus-trates this criterion.

Incorrect:	Under $10,000
	$10,000–$20,000
	$20,000–$30,000
	$30,000–$40,000
	$40,000–$50,000
	Over $50,000
Correct:	Under $10,000
	$10,000–$19,999
	$20,000–$29,999
	$30,000–$39,999
	$40,000–$49,999
	$50,000 or more

• Arrange questions logically and use branching techniques, if neces-sary, to help respondents avoid irrelevant questions.

Branching techniques are demonstrated in items B.1.a and B.1.d of the observation form shown in Figure 1.2. Item C of the form also leaves additional space for the observer's comments.

OBSERVATION — COMPETITOR GROCERY STORE

Name of Grocery Observed: _____

Address: _____

Date of Observation: _____ Start time: _____ End time: _____

Visit the assigned location on a weekday between 10 a.m. and 1:30 p.m. Your objective is to observe the cleanliness of the facility, adequacy of stock, variety of stock, and interaction of store employees with customers.

A. Exterior Evaluation

When you arrive at the site, evaluate the parking lot and exterior signage before entering the store.

1. Was the number of parking spaces adequate? Yes_____ No _____

2. Were the sidewalks and parking areas free of debris? Yes_____ No _____

3. Was the store easily identifiable from the parking lot? Yes_____ No_____

4. Were windows and doors clean? Yes_____ No _____

5. Were posters or announcements in the windows appealing in appearance? Yes_____ No_____ Not Applicable _____

B. Interior Evaluation

After observing the exterior features, enter the store. Acquire a cart and begin shopping by going up and down the aisles. **Without disturbing anyone,** walk through the facility, checking all items noted on this observation form. If you are unable to complete any item, mark it with red ink.

1. **Café area**

(a) Was there a café for patrons to sit and enjoy beverage/food? Yes _____ No _____ **(if No, go to 2.)**

(b) Was there a variety of beverages available (more than just coffee)? Yes _____ No _____

(c) Was there a menu of breakfast or lunch items? Yes _____ No_____

(d) Was there a restroom in the café area? Yes_____ No_____ **(if No, go to 1.g.)**

(e) Was the restroom supplied with towels and soap? Yes_____ No_____

(f) Was the restroom clean and fresh? Yes_____ No_____

(g) Were customers using the café area? Yes_____ No _____

2. Aisles

(a) Were the aisles clean and unobstructed? Yes_____ No _____

(b) Were products arranged with labels clearly visible? Yes_____ No _____

(c) Were two carts able to pass the same point in the aisles? Yes_____ No _____

3. Products

(a) Was there an adequate supply of products on shelves (no empty locations)? Yes_____ No _____

(b) Were there specialty products (ethnic, diabetic, and so forth) on the shelves? Yes_____ No _____

4. Employee interaction

Ask an employee for help to find ketchup. **Do not interrupt anyone who is talking with another employee or customer.** If you have waited at least 10 minutes and no employee has assisted you, you may leave the facility without completing question 4a-c. Report that fact in Part C Explanations.

(a) Was the employee polite? Yes_____ No _____

(b) Did the employee walk you to the ketchup? Yes_____ No _____

(c) Did the employee ask if he/she could help you further? Yes_____ No _____

C. **Explanations.** Use this area to explain any item to which you answered "No." Identify the item and give a brief explanation.

D. **Conclusion.**

Within 12 hours of completing this observation, log into your account at www.westudy.com and complete the online version of the observation form. Keep this paper copy in your files for a minimum of 6 months.

Figure 1.2 Observation form

Instructions

The instrument must contain clear, complete instructions to the user. Instructions must indicate how to complete the instrument and what to do with it after completion. Even a simple checklist, must contain clear instructions (see Figure 1.3).

Our Grocer Store Visitor's Checklist

Your answers to this survey will help Our Grocery Store plan its products and services.

A. Have you visited this store before today?

   Yes _____ No _____

B. Whether you have or have not visited this store, please check any items that you *currently* associate with Our Grocery Store.

1. Good prices	1. _____
2. Clean store	2. _____
3. Good selection	3. _____
4. Fresh produce	4. _____
5. Nice café	5. _____
6. Friendly people	6. _____
7. Easy to get to	7. _____

Please leave this checklist with your cashier.

Thank you for participating in this survey. We wish you a pleasant and safe trip.

Figure 1.3 Checklist

In addition, the researcher should define any terms or scale values that may be interpreted in different ways, as is demonstrated in the opening instructions of Figure 1.4, where adult is defined as a person who appears to be age 18 or older. Ambiguity must be avoided in instructions as well as in questions.

Interview Guide

Perceptions of Our Grocery Store

_____   _____   _____
Location of interview   Date of interview   Interviewer's initials

INSTRUCTIONS: Approach an adult (an individual who appears to be 18 or older) who is seated in the café, in the aisles, or in the parking lot in which you are conducting the survey. After greeting the individual, explain the study briefly. For example, "I'm trying to find out what people know about our grocery store."

A. **Ask:** *Will you answer a few questions about this store?*

   No _____ Offer one of our store newspaper ads, thank the individual, and end the conversation cordially.

   Yes _____ Go to item B.

B. **Ask:** *Do you live within 10 miles from this site?*

   No _____ Explain that we need participants who live within 10 miles for our survey. Offer one of our store ads and end the conversation cordially.

   Yes _____ Go to item C.

C. **Say:** *We are trying to stratify our sample by age. Into what age range do you fit?*

   18–34 _____ 35–54 _____ 55+ _____

D. Indicate the participant's gender: Male ____ Female ____

F. **Say:** *I now have just six questions for you.* Read each question clearly and slowly enough for the interviewee to understand the question and answer options.

   1. What is the primary reason for your trip to this store today?

      Large shopping trip   _____

      Pick up today's groceries   _____

      Pick up one or two items   _____

      Going to café   _____

      Other   _____

2

2. Have you visited this store before?

Yes_____ How often within the past three years? _____

No _____

3. Why did you choose to visit this store? (More than one answer may be given.)

Recommended by family or friend   _____

Closest to home   _____

Carries one specific item not available elsewhere _____

Responded to advertising   _____

Other _____

4. What other stores in this area have you visited?

None _____

Stores cited _____

5. How much have you spent or plan to spend today?

up to $10   _____

$10.01 - $30.00   _____

$30.01 - $50.00   _____

$50.01 - $100.00   _____

$100.01 or more   _____

6. **Say:** *Thanks for your assistance. Here's the store's current ad with a number of useful coupons and sales. Enjoy your visit to our store.*

Return all interview guides to Our Grocery Store office at the end of each working day.

Figure 1.4 Interview guide

If the instrument is complicated or lengthy, the instructions should be broken into understandable units. For each new section of the instrument, meaningful headings or instructions related to that section should be provided. (Note the observer instructions in Figure 1.2 and the interviewee instructions in Figure 1.4.) When a rating scale is used, it should be repeated at the top of each page to which it applies so that users need not turn back to check the scale values. Many respondents will not expend that effort; they may, instead, supply inaccurate responses.

To ensure that the instructions for returning an instrument are not lost or misplaced, they should appear on the instrument itself, not in a separate letter or instruction sheet. (See the specific directions at the end of Figures 1.2, to 1.4.) Even when an addressed return envelope is provided, the instrument itself should show the address to which it must be returned. Figure 1.5, the last page of a paper questionnaire, includes an address for returning it.

---

7. If the cruise terminal is relocated:
   ____ I anticipate no change in my quality of life.
   ____ My quality of life may decline.
   ____ My quality of life will very likely decline.

8. **Please provide some information about yourself to help us process the answers to this survey.**

   - Your age range is:
     Under 25____   26-35____   36-45____   46-55____   56-65____   Over 65____

   - You are:
     Female ____   Male____

   - Your profession or occupation is best categorized as:

___ Advertising, media, marketing, and public relations	___ Hospitality and leisure services
___ Artistic endeavors	___ Legal services
___ Banking, economics, and financial services	___ Manufacturing
___ Business, management, and human resources	___ Public sector, politics, and policy
___ Consulting	___ Real estate services
___ Development and non-governmental not-for-profit	___ Retail
___ Education and religious services	___ Technology
___ Energy and environment	___ Transportation
___ Engineering and construction services	___ Wholesale distribution
___ Healthcare services	___ Retired
___ Homemaker (Full-Time)	___ Other: _____

Please return your completed questionnaire to:

South Carolina State Ports Authority
P. O. Box 22288
Charleston, SC 29413

Figure 1.5 Questionnaire page with return instructions

Envelopes can easily be lost, making response impossible if the questionnaire itself does not contain the address.

Although instructions tell respondents what to do with an instrument, the instrument itself must be presented to potential participants in such a way that they are motivated to respond. An effective transmittal message accomplishes that objective. No survey instrument should be distributed without a transmittal message, either contained in a separate message or placed on the instrument itself.

Guides for Transmittal Messages

An effective transmittal message builds researcher–subject rapport and motivates subjects to participate in the research. A transmittal message may be written, as in a cover letter that accompanies a printed questionnaire or an e-mail that accompanies an online questionnaire; or the transmittal message may be spoken, as in an opening conversation with interviewees. In all situations, the message must be planned so that it will reveal enough information to stimulate interest and motivation without biasing responses, as shown in Figure 1.6.

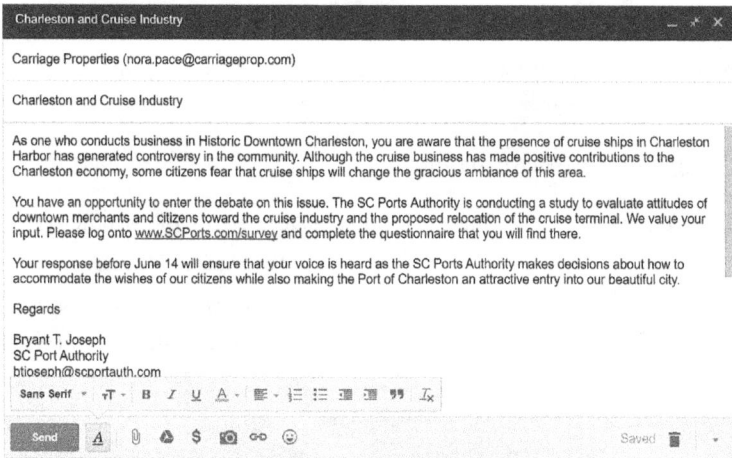

Figure 1.6 Transmittal message in e-mail format

The following guides will help you develop effective transmittal messages.

- Use an interesting opening that focuses on the receiver, not the sender of the message. When possible, identify a reader interest or need that may provide motivation to participate.
- Provide enough identifying information to legitimize your request. That information may include the purpose of the study, the company or agency for which it is being conducted, how the information will be used, and potential benefits of the study.
- Indicate the role of the participants and the protections that are extended to them. Role definition may include explanation of how participants were selected and what is requested of them (for example, 5 minutes of your time, answers to 10 questions, etc.). Protection usually includes assurance of confidentiality, particularly if sensitive information is sought.
- Specify exactly what is required (for example, complete the questionnaire and mail it before August 15), and make that action as easy as possible. Enclosing a stamped, addressed envelope with a mail survey or asking short, clearly worded questions in a telephone survey are ways to make responses easy.

After the instrument and transmittal message have been developed, a two-step task remains before they are ready for use: testing and revision.

Testing and Revising Instruments

The objective of *instrument testing* is to detect errors or weaknesses in all aspects of the instrument before it is used. Instructions, questions, response modes, sequence of items, format, and level of language should be scrutinized. Ideally, two kinds of testing are used: in-house and field testing.

In-house testing involves presenting the instrument to colleagues or other impartial critics for their evaluation. To evaluate all aspects of the instrument, those critics should be knowledgeable about instrument design and about the kinds of data that are to be collected. Such evaluators can often detect shortcomings and provide suggestions for instrument revision.

In addition, the instrument should be presented to these critics in the same form (paper or computer screen) as it will be presented to actual participants. For example, critics would use the link in the transmittal e-mail (Figure 1.6) to test the online questionnaire shown in Figure 1.7.

Charleston and the Cruise Industry

Please share what you know and think about the impact of the cruise industry in Charleston.

1. Approximately how many jobs in the Charleston area are supported by the cruise industry?

- ○ 500
- ○ 400
- ○ 300
- ○ 200
- ○ 100

2. Approximately how much economic output (in millions) is generated by the cruise industry in Charleston?

- ○ $55 million
- ○ $45 million
- ○ $35 million
- ○ $25 million
- ○ $15 million

3. Which of the following conditions do you associate with the presence of a cruise ship in port? (Check all that apply.)

- ○ Abrasive interactions with cruise passengers.
- ○ Decreased pedestrian traffic in neighborhood.
- ○ Decreased sales of food, lodging, and/or merchandise and services.
- ○ Environmental/noise pollution.
- ○ Increased pedestrian traffic in neighborhood.
- ○ Increased sales of food, lodging, and/or merchandise and services.
- ○ Pleasant interactions with cruise passengers.
- ○ Reluctance to leave home or place of business.
- ○ Smooth flow of vehicular traffic.
- ○ Traffic jams.
- ○ Other (Please describe.)

4. One option the Ports Authority is considering is to relocate the cruise terminal to a point somewhat north of Union Pier. At this time, do you favor or oppose relocation of the cruise terminal to this site? (Check one.)

- ○ Favor Go to Item 5
- ○ Oppose Go to Item 7

5. Relocating the cruise terminal is projected to bring approximately 350 jobs to the Charleston region and contribute $45 million to the local economy during the 12 months of construction. Which of the following statements best reflects your attitude about those projections?

- ○ Projections are guesses, not facts.
- ○ The Charleston area needs that kind of economic boost; let's do it.
- ○ The Charleston historic district will receive little of that benefit.
- ○ The Charleston historic district will likely share in that benefit.

Figure 1.7 Online questionnaire

Figure 1.7 Online questionnaire (continued)

Field testing involves presenting the instrument to a group of respondents typical of those with whom it will eventually be used. One way to do a field test is to ask potential participants to complete the instrument without informing them that they are a test group. After they have completed the instrument, the test group should then be asked to provide additional information about the effectiveness of the instrument—its clarity, format, time requirement, and so forth. Discussion of the respondents' reactions to the questionnaire will frequently yield valuable suggestions for instrument revision.

In the future, you will undoubtedly use online surveys comparable to the one in Figure 1.7 more frequently than traditional paper-and-pencil instruments (Figure 1.5). You have many websites to choose from when creating and distributing a questionnaire online. When choosing a survey host, consider these three factors.

- *Choose a site that is mobile friendly.* Because of the widespread use of mobile devices, make sure that your online questionnaire is as easy to read and complete on a tablet or phone as on a desktop computer or laptop.
- *Select a site that offers a variety of distribution options.* Determine whether your survey can be embedded in respondents' websites or posted to a social network in addition to e-mail distribution.

Pick a website that accommodates users with disabilities. Examples include access to screen readers for blind or visually impaired users to read displayed text by means of a text-to-speech synthesizer or Braille display and audio descriptions of visuals, including videos. Note: Look for the term Section 508 compliant or W3C compliant. Section 508 refers to information technology (IT) requirements specified in the U.S. Rehabilitation Act and W3C refers to IT standards set by the World Wide Web Consortium.[2] The partial questionnaire in Figure 1.7 was created in SurveyMonkey (www.surveymonkey.com), which offers three professional (subscription) versions and a free version (limited to 10 questions and 100 respondents). It includes a mobile app and collaboration features.

The following list contains a few alternatives for creating and distributing web-based surveys. These websites include editable templates or the option of designing your own questionnaire.

- *QuestionPro* (www.questionpro.com) boasts full multilingual support, tablet and mobile phone apps, and a free version along with subscription service.
- *Lime Survey* (www.limesurvey.org), a free, Open Source program, allows integration of pictures and videos into questionnaires. It also provides a printable survey version, and it complies with W3C standards.
- *KeySurvey* (www.keysurvey.com), known as enterprise application software (EAS), is designed to satisfy the needs of an entire organization, rather than individual users. Therefore, a free version is unavailable.
- *Google Forms* (www.google.com/forms) has been streamlined for viewing and editing on mobile devices. Users can insert headers and page breaks.
- *GetFeedback* (www.getfeedback.com) offers a 14-day free trial. It identifies as mobile friendly and boasts collaboration features for team research projects.
- *Formstack* (www.formstack.com) contains forms that comply with Section 508. It also accommodates an approval workflow, a business processes that involves sending a document or item to colleagues or managers for approval. This software manages and tracks the human tasks involved with the process and provides a record of the completed process.

Collecting Primary Data

Methods to obtain information from primary sources are either active or passive. *Passive data collection* involves observation of characteristics of the people or actions that are the elements of analysis; the person collecting the data records them on an observation form comparable to the one illustrated in Figure 1.2 but does not interact or communicate with those subjects. *Active data collection*, such as interviewing, involves questioning the subjects; the person collecting the data interacts with the subjects who actively supply data to the researcher.

Passive Methods

Passive data collection methods used by business researchers include search of company records, observation, and some forms of experimentation.

Search of Company Records

Company records contain much information generated during daily operations. Personnel, production, marketing, credit, accounting, and finance records are accumulated and modified daily. Those records are often used in day-to-day decisions and subsequently stored for possible future use. Although some of the information may be made available to the public in an annual report or a publicity release, much of the material is never published and distributed externally. But as new problems or challenges arise within the organization, the data that have been accumulated in the files often provide a perspective on the problems and information to solve them.

Company records are often the first primary data source consulted by a business researcher. Some researchers consider company records to be superior to other primary data sources for two reasons:

- The data are objective. The data were generated for purposes other than the immediate report that is being prepared.
- The data are economical to use. Collecting data from company files is generally the least expensive method of gathering primary data.

Company files are especially useful when the research requires historical data about some aspect of the company's operations. For example, data from personnel files will show changes in the composition of the company's labor force; data from customer service files can identify a possible flaw in product design; and data from files in the information technology assistance center may be able to identify emerging user needs. When company records cannot provide adequate valid data, however, other strategies must be used.

Many companies store information about company activity in computerized databases and digitized files. A *database* is a collection of related records stored in a computer file. For example, a customer database might contain such information as name, street or post office address, city, state, ZIP code, telephone number, e-mail address, and account number. Your store may have collected some or all of this type of information as customers sign up for the "special shopper" discount card. A record is all of the information about one person or organization. Each category of information within the record is called a field. In this example, there would be eight fields: name, street or post office address, city, state, ZIP code, telephone number, e-mail address, and account number. A digitized file, on the other hand, might consist of text and graphics. A proposal received via electronic mail, a sales report, a memo reporting the decisions at a meeting, and a status report of a project are examples of the types of documents stored as digitized files.

When information processing systems are integrated, personal computers are linked to other equipment so that information can be accessed by all authorized users. In an integrated system, you can relatively easily collect and process information that is stored in a database. You must first obtain authority to use the file, then gain access to the appropriate file, identify the correct record, identify the categories of data desired, and direct the computer to find the data. You can then organize the data in many ways: alphabetically or numerically, ascending or descending order, or by any category of information stored in the file. You can also sort the accounts alphabetically or by the date of the last usage of the discount shopper card.

Observation

A second passive method is *observation*. In this technique, the researcher (or a mechanical or electronic device) watches the data sources and records information about the elements that are being analyzed.

Assume, for example, that productivity is lower than average among the employees of one supervisor in a computer tech support call center. You may decide to collect data about working patterns of those employees. Company records are not likely to contain that information, except to the extent that it has been recorded in performance reviews. Asking employees about working patterns is unlikely to yield valid data because the technicians may be unwilling or unable to report how they work. Therefore, observation of the employees performing their tasks may be the best data collection method. In your observation, you could record several behaviors: how quickly they begin work after arrival, how they organize their work stations, how much call time is spent on "chitchat" with the customer versus how much is spent on solving the technical problem, the degree of direct supervision they receive, how they respond to the supervisor's comments, the percentage of time they are away from their work stations, and so on.

In some situations, observation can be accomplished mechanically. For example, in your store, you have scanners that read and record every item purchased. These data are entered into your inventory and sales records. If the customer uses a shopper discount card, you also know what that individual buys during each visit.

Experimentation

Observation is often an integral part of another method, experimentation. *Experimentation* may employ both passive and active data collection methods. Assume that, as part of a wellness program, a company's dietician wants to encourage employees to eat fresh fruits and vegetables. You are assigned the task of determining how to increase employee consumption of those foods in the company cafeteria. In cooperation with the cafeteria staff, you decide to conduct an experiment in which you manipulate the location of the fruits and vegetables in the cafeteria layout. Then you observe employees' behaviors (looking at fruits and vegetables, not looking at them, selecting, not selecting, and so on) as they go through the line. That observation is a passive method. But you may supplement it with an active method, asking employees why they did or did not choose a fresh fruit or vegetable.

A major shortcoming of observation is that the observer must interpret what he or she sees, and different observers may assign different meanings to events. In the cafeteria experiment, for example, when an employee pauses in front of the fruits and vegetables, one observer may interpret that behavior as noticing the display. Another observer may interpret the behavior as a delay caused by other factors, such as a slowdown somewhere on the line. When an employee selects an item from the display, the observer might be tempted to assume that the decision was made at that time and was influenced by the attractiveness of the display. But the employee may have decided several hours earlier to eat an apple or a salad for lunch. Because of such potential shortcomings in observation, that method is often supplemented by an active method.

Active Methods: Traditional and Online

Active methods, also called communication methods, involve questioning subjects. Questioning is an appropriate data collection method when the information you need consists of knowledge, attitudes, opinions, or beliefs. In many situations, questioning is the only way to obtain necessary data. You can, for example, get data from personnel files about employee participation in a 401(k) plan, but you cannot determine employee attitudes toward the company's contribution to the plan from those files. Attitudes must be determined by questioning the employees. After the questioning, the results may be compiled and stored in company files, but those data then become historical data. Attitudes could change dramatically within a short time if company policy or economic conditions change.

Questioning can be accomplished by either personal or impersonal means. Interviewing is a personal means, whereas using questionnaires and electronic surveys tends to be impersonal.[23]

Interviews

In an interview, the researcher or an assistant orally presents instructions and questions to the subjects and records their answers. Interviews may be face-to-face or mediated.

The *face-to-face interview* is a rich communication medium that allows both the interviewer and the respondent to interpret nonverbal cues as well as oral questions. For example, the respondent can ask for clarification of a question he or she does not understand. Likewise, the interviewer can use probes to encourage deeper thought if the responses seem superficial. Such richness may improve rapport between the researcher and the subject, thereby encouraging openness; but that same richness may stimulate the respondent to give socially acceptable answers, thereby biasing the data.

In a *mediated interview*, such as a phone interview, the participants cannot see one another. Thus, trust and rapport must be established through oral means. Phone interviews are considered by some researchers to be equal or perhaps superior to other active primary data collection methods in obtaining valid data, particularly when the subject matter is sensitive. For example, respondents may be more willing to answer questions about personal health matters in the relative anonymity of a phone interview than in a face-to-face interview. Phone interviews have been particularly successful in business-to-business situations because respondents may be willing to give a few minutes of phone time when they are not willing to schedule an appointment for an interview.

The inability to show prompts, display materials, or present a long list of options is a severe limitation of phone interviews. Another major disadvantage of phone interviews is the increasing consumer resistance to that method of intrusion for marketing purposes.

Interviews may be structured or unstructured. In a *structured interview*, the interviewer follows a formal guide that provides the exact wording of instructions and questions as well as the exact sequence in which questions are to be asked. If interviewers follow the guide as written, all subjects will be questioned in essentially the same manner. In an *unstructured interview*, the interviewer uses either no formalized questions or very loosely structured ones. The objective is to get the respondent to talk freely about the interview topic.

Today, researchers use computer assistance in both face-to-face and phone interviews. For example, in phone surveys, questions may be presented by a voice recording; the subject is asked to respond by pressing designated digits on the phone keypad. Or a computer may be set up to provide an interviewer with a questionnaire and a means of recording responses. A particular advantage of this technique is the ability to branch easily to different paths in the interview, depending on a respondent's answer. Calculations can also be programmed into the questionnaire, enabling the interviewer to ask a simple question, such as how many glasses of milk each family member consumes daily, and immediately convert the answer into annual family consumption. Another advantage is the ability to randomize or rotate a series of questions. In a face-to-face interview, the computer can also present visual stimuli.

Focus Group Interviews

Focus group interviews are often used to determine interest in a new product or service, the effectiveness of advertising and communications research, background studies on consumers' frames of reference, or consumer attitudes and behaviors toward an idea, organization, and so on.

The standard focus group interview involves 6 to 12 similar individuals, such as male customers, a young professionals group, or those who regularly purchase a certain laundry detergent, who are brought together to discuss a particular topic. The respondents are selected according to the relevant sampling plan and meet at a central location that has equipment to make an audio or audiovisual record of the discussion. A moderator or facilitator is present to keep the discussion moving and focused on the topic, but otherwise the sessions are free flowing. The competent moderator attempts to develop three clear stages in a 1- to 3-hour interview:

1. Establish rapport with the group, structure the rules of the group interaction, and set objectives.
2. Pose questions to provoke intense discussion in relevant areas.
3. Summarize the group's responses to determine the extent of agreement.

Usually the moderator also analyzes the transcript or recording of the session and prepares a summary of the meeting. Focus groups can generate much data in a relatively short period. When little is known in advance of an investigation, the focus group may provide a basis for formulating research questions and problems.

Questionnaire Surveys

In a questionnaire, or self-completion survey, printed instructions and questions are presented to the subjects on paper or on a website, and the subjects record their answers as directed on the questionnaire.

Questionnaire surveys are attractive to investigators for three reasons:

- The cost is low, relative to the amount of data that can be collected in one survey.
- The large geographic area from which the researcher can draw the sample may improve data validity.
- The assurance of anonymity and lack of pressure while the respondent completes the questionnaire contribute to data validity.

Response rates to questionnaire surveys are relatively low, however. Response rates can be influenced by questionnaire design. To increase response rates—and, thereby, data validity—researchers often offer inducements to the subjects. Market researchers have identified the relative effectiveness of various inducements as show in Figure 1.8.

Inducement	Influence
Pre-notification	Increase in response
Personalization	Increase in response
Monetary incentives	Increase in response
Follow-up	Increase in response
Return postage	Increase in response
Sponsorship	Increase in response if subject identifies with sponsor
Appeal in cover letter	Ego, science, or social utility appeals tend to be most effective
Specification of deadline	No influence on number of returns; may accelerate speed of returns

Figure 1.8 Comparison of questionnaire response inducements

Studies have shown that web-based questionnaires, when skillfully designed, are completed more quickly than phone, face-to-face, and paper questionnaire surveys. This medium also allows presentation of visual images, longer lists of options, and easy branching strategies. By involving the participant visually and manually, this medium tends to maintain the respondents' attention and promotes good-quality data to the end of the questionnaire.

Comparison of Active and Passive Methods

Your choice of a data collection method must be based on its ability to obtain accurate data and satisfy other relevant research criteria. Factors that often influence the success of a project are the ability to identify subjects or to ensure subject anonymity, flexibility of the data-gathering technique, ability of the technique to tap sensitive data, protecting the data from researcher influence, scheduling requirements, time requirements, probable response rate, and cost.

If your research design requires that subjects be identified, a search of company records, observation, or personal interview would be an excellent technique, as shown in Figure 1.9.

On the other hand, if you wish to ensure subject anonymity, a search of company records or a personal interview would be a poor technique. Similarly, if you are concerned about the accuracy of sensitive data, you should choose the records search technique or a survey as opposed to observation or personal interviews. Some sensitive data, such as information about contributions to a political party or personal health practices, cannot be collected by observation and may be distorted in an interview. By weighing the relative importance of the nine dimensions, you can select a technique that best meets the requirements of your research project.

After selecting your data collection method or methods, you must design a way to capture the data and make them available for analysis. (Note: Online survey services automate the distribution of surveys and the recording of responses, as well as data analysis, reporting, and charting. Data analysis is the subject of Chapter 2.) The precision of your data collection instruments will greatly influence the quality of your data.

			Methods			
Dimensions	**Search of Records**	**Observation**	**Personal Interview**	**Focus Group Interview**	**Questionnaire Survey**	**Electronic Survey**
Subject identification	Excellent	Excellent*	Excellent	Excellent*	Fair	Excellent*
Flexibility	Excellent	Good to fair	Excellent	Excellent	Fair	Poor
Subject anonymity	Fair to poor	Excellent*	Poor	Excellent*	Excellent*	Excellent*
Accuracy of sensitive data	Excellent	Fair	Fair	Fair	Good	Excellent
Control of researcher effects	Good	Poor	Poor	Poor	Excellent	Excellent
Flexibility of scheduling	Excellent	Fair	Poor	Fair	Excellent	Good
Time required	Good	Fair	Fair	Fair	Fair	Excellent
Probable response rate	Good	Good	Good	Good	Fair to poor	Good
Cost	Excellent	Fair	Poor	Fair	Good	Good

*Dependent on design of study; subject identification or anonymity can be planned.

Figure 1.9 Comparison of primary data collection methods

Teamwork and Primary Data

Collaborative writing often consists of a combination of collective and independent work, depending on the stage of the project. While collaboration is recommended during the planning, data evaluation, and final draft stages, independent work is recommended in the data collection and analysis stage.

Together, the team should identify possible data sources. If the research requires the use of primary data, one or two members of the team might be responsible for designing the questionnaires or interview guides, but all members should participate in a critical review of those instruments before they are used. During the data-collection phase, it may be efficient for team members to function independently, each person collecting and interpreting data for the segment of the study for which he or she is responsible.

After the data are collected and analyzed, the group should again work together to plan the report draft. Members should discuss the data, evaluate its adequacy, and agree on its interpretation. At this time, the team should also review the report outline (planning phase) and adjust it as necessary.

Summary

Research is a complex process. However, it does not have to be complicated. When we identify a problem or opportunity and want to know how we could best proceed, a research project may provide the best suggestions. We first would want to be sure we clearly understand the problem we are facing. That means that we must look at it from several angles or viewpoints to ensure that we are not merely addressing a simple symptom, but the real problem. Next, we want to gather as much data as practical about the problem. Some will believe that we can never have too much data. However, there can be a problem with "analysis paralysis" in that we fear making decisions for not having enough data. At some point, it becomes necessary to make decisions on the data and analysis we have. We can make the data collection and analysis somewhat simpler by ensuring that we have data from a representative sample of cases of the entire possibility, whether that's customer information or observations of naturally occurring phenomena. Once we have a sampling, we can subject the collected data to scrutiny in a variety of forms. It may be helpful to use this checklist when planning business research.

❑ Decide what you want to know.
- ○ What is the problem you see (versus symptoms)?
- ○ What are possibilities that are not yet met?
- ○ What ideas do you have to resolve the problem; for example, ideas that might make your grocery store customers happier or more loyal?

❑ Determine what questions will best elicit valid and reliable answers to the question(s).
- ○ How can I ask the questions that will provide quality answers?
- ○ What can I put into my questions that will ensure people want to answer them?
- ○ How can I be sure that the questions I ask will be consistently answered?

❑ Define a sample that is indicative of the entire population you are considering.
- ○ For example, who are my current customers?
- ○ What are their characteristics that may influence answers?
- ○ How many people do I need to survey or observe?

❑ Develop a method to deploy the questions in observation, interview, or questionnaire.
- ○ What is the best method to get the questions in front of the sample?
- ○ How can I entice the sample to respond?
- ○ Am I asking only those questions that this sample needs to answer?

❑ Design a test of the questions, sample, and method.
- ○ Who do I trust in house to give me good feedback on my research project so far?

○ Is there an easy group of customers with whom I can field test to see if my questions really elicit quality answers?

❑ Gather data using the selected instrument.

Following these steps may seem daunting at first; but with thought and practice, these procedures will become second nature—and valuable to any research project you undertake.

CHAPTER 2

Analyzing Business Research Data

Alan R. Belcher, PhD

Ashford University.

In this chapter, we discuss how to analyze research data once it is collected for a project. Following up on the scenario in Case 1.1, where you own and manage Our Grocery Store, you collected data from many customers about their anticipated needs. You are confident that you have collected adequate data in a form that will be easily analyzed. You believe that the questions you asked were the right questions and that you received truthful answers from the people who responded.

So how do we go about analyzing this data to make meaning from it? Data analysis is the entire process of converting raw data into meaningful information for decision-makers. Analysis is a process of data reduction: the mass of raw data is reduced to classes or sets of information, those sets are reduced to major findings, and ultimately the findings are interpreted to yield conclusions and recommendations. Case 2.1 is an example of how data reduction works.

In this chapter, we will use the data set shown in Figure 2.1 to further explain the data reduction process.

Figure 2.1 shows only a portion of the data but will give you an idea of the type of data contained in the full data set. Through surveys of customers who come into the store over a period of 6 days, we collected information from 564 customers. For each customer, we know the age,

Case 2.1

Data Reduction: An Example

You will conduct research to identify potential sites for a new grocery store. Your data collection activities will yield many facts, which might include demographic data, responses to a consumer survey, and data about building sites currently on the market.

- Your data analysis will require classification of the data into meaningful groups that will permit you to compare the desirability of different sites. One category could be the demographics of defined sections of the city.
- Facts about each area—population growth, average household income, effective buying power, new home construction, and so on—can be reduced to major findings. Those findings would include the area that has shown the fastest growth in population, has the highest average household income, has the greatest effective buying power, and has had the most new-home construction during a defined period.
- Major findings may be reduced further into a summary statement identifying one section of the city that demonstrates the greatest economic vitality. Similar data reduction would be required for the facts gathered in your consumer survey and the information about available building sites.
- The summary statement often can be reduced to a single recommendation, though you began with hundreds of facts. Assume these findings:
  - A revitalized section of the central city shows the greatest economic vitality.
  - Consumers in the revitalized area expressed the greatest desire for a conveniently located supermarket.
  - A building site is available in an appropriate location and at an affordable price.

Your one recommendation would likely be that the company purchase the specified site for a new supermarket.

	A	B	C	D	E	F	G	H	I	J	K	L	M	N	O	P	Q	R	S
	Respondent #	Age	Gender	# in household	Income up to $20K	Income between $20K and $40K	Income between $40K and $60K	Income $60K or more	Income scale	Live within 10 miles	Online shopping	Quick lunch	Wi-fi	Senior discount	Home delivery	Avg. weekly amount spent			
1																			
2	1	62	0	6	0	0	0	1	4	1	5	1	5	5	5	194			
3	2	32	0	5	0	0	0	1	4	1	5	2	5	3	5	13			
4	3	65	1	3	0	0	1	0	3	1	1	2	2	5	2	92			
5	4	18	1	2	0	1	0	0	2	1	3	2	5	3	4	163			
6	5	34	0	3	0	0	1	0	3	1	1	3	5	5	2	183			
7	6	84	1	4	0	0	0	1	4	1	3	3	4	5	5	214			
8	7	58	0	5	0	0	0	1	4	1	5	3	5	5	5	174			
9	--	--	--	--	--	--	--	--	--	--	--	--	--	--	--	--			
10	560	70	1	6	0	0	0	1	4	1	5	2	3	5	5	49			
11	561	64	1	3	0	0	1	0	3	1	1	3	3	5	2	134			
12	562	42	0	3	0	0	1	0	3	0	2	3	4	2	5	143			
13	563	78	1	1	1	0	0	0	1	1	1	3	2	5	4	128			
14	564	34	0	5	0	0	0	1	4	1	5	3	5	3	5	60			
15																			
16																			
17																			

Figure 2.1 Part of a data set

number of individuals in the household, the household income range, whether the individual lives within 10 miles of the store, the individual's gender, how much the person typically spends each week, and his or her preference of five possible new services on a scale of 1 (not desired) to 5 (very much desired).

Preparing Primary Data for Analysis

For most types of contemporary business research, data preparation includes editing and coding.

Editing

Editing is inspection of the data to detect errors and omissions. Editing is done to ensure that data are accurate, consistent, complete, and arranged in a way that facilitates coding or classification.

Some editing can be done during or immediately after collection. For example, an interviewer should check the interview guide immediately after an interview to determine whether all items have been covered and whether any obvious inconsistencies exist. If an item has been omitted, the interviewer may be able to schedule a prompt follow-up interview and get the necessary information. If the interviewer notices inconsistencies in a respondent's answers, those items may also be reviewed in a follow-up interview. If inconsistencies cannot be resolved, you may have to eliminate that respondent's data from your analysis.

Data collected by questionnaire must be edited after all questionnaires have been returned. Your objective is to detect missing answers and unusable (illegible or obviously inconsistent) responses. In some instances, you may be able to supply the correct information, as when a person provides annual instead of monthly income. In other situations, you may be able to determine the correct answer by a follow-up contact with the survey participant. Frequently, however, missing or unusable answers must be coded and handled as such.

How to deal with missing or incomplete data should not be an arbitrary decision. To protect the validity and reliability of data, the research design should include a decision about how to handle such data. For example, the research design might indicate that the number of missing or unusable answers will be reported for each item; but the findings will be based on usable answers.

Coding

Coding is the process of assigning numerals or other symbols to answers so that they can be categorized and interpreted, possibly statistically. Questionnaires and interview guides can be designed to eliminate the need for extensive manual coding. Closed questions, in particular, can be set up so that the responses are numbered with appropriate codes. Open-ended questions must be coded manually to fit into categories defined by the researchers. Any coding system used to establish categories of information must meet four criteria: appropriate, exhaustive, mutually exclusive, and one-dimensional.

Appropriate

As with all aspects of analysis, coding must be directed by the problem and purpose. Those factors, for example, must determine whether age or income ranges should be narrow or wide and how many scale points (values) should be used to measure responses. The following codes and ranges might be appropriate to measure annual earned income of students at a state university.

Code and category	Income ranges
1	$0–$9,999.99
2	$10,000–$19,999.99
3	$20,000–$29,999.99
4	$30,000–$39,999.99
5	$40,000 or more

However, these codes and ranges are likely inappropriate to measure income of faculty members at that institution because a disproportionate number would fall into category 5.

Exhaustive

The classification set must capture the full range of information. The set used in the previous example will provide little useful information about university professors' salaries. If the majority of responses fall into category 5, the only information acquired is that the majority of the faculty earns at least US$40,000 annually.

Responses to open-ended questions must also be coded to identify the richness of the data. A question about plans for postsecondary education, for example, may originally have been grouped into three sets: college, technical school, no plans for postsecondary education. Closer examination of the data, however, may suggest the need for more classifications to identify the many dimensions of college and technical school education that the responses have indicated: religious-based college, community college, technical school, proprietary trade school, state college, private college, state university, private university, and so on.

Mutually Exclusive

The classifications must not overlap. This standard is met when an answer can be placed in only one category. In an occupational survey, the classifications may be professional, managerial, technical, sales, clerical, and operative. However, a nurse who supervises two assistants in a company health center may have difficulty choosing between the professional and managerial categories. It may also be possible, when having multiple options, that the survey is created so that respondents may mark more than one answer. This is often phrased as a question with the notation, "Mark all that apply." In this case, the total number of answers may be more than the number of respondents, resulting in a question with more than 100% response rate. In the previous example of student income ranges, each category is mutually exclusive. A respondent whose income falls near an extreme end of a category, such as US$19,999, should have no difficulty selecting the appropriate category.

One-Dimensional

All items in a classification set must be related to the same concept. In a question asking what kind of automobile the respondent owns or leases, the responses may be subcompact, compact, intermediate, standard, full, premium, and none. The first six items refer to one dimension, car size, but the last item deals with another dimension, current ownership status. That item is best handled in a separate category, perhaps as a screening question, such as "Do you currently own or lease an automobile?"

In the data set shown in Figure 2.1 (page 53), the data were coded to create numerical scales for each item. For instance, the respondent number and the age of the individual could be input without additional coding or transformation. The gender would have been collected and recorded as "M" or "F"; however, it is coded numerically such that a "1" represents a female while a "0" represents a male. In the income ranges, an "X" was entered on the survey form. The "X" has been replaced with a "1" and blanks have been substituted with a "0." Converting data items to numeric values makes the analysis much simpler when using either a spreadsheet or statistical software.

Data Analysis Requirements

To enhance the accuracy of your analysis, you must understand the research problem, maintain a critical mindset, apply logical thinking, and understand basic statistical procedures.

Understand the Research Problem

Reviewing the research problem and purpose will remind you of what stimulated the research and of the objectives to be met by the study. Assume the following research problem and purpose.

> *Research Problem:* To determine new services to be provided by Our Grocery Store.
>
> *Purpose:* To acquire data from current customers, finding out their desires for a range of possible new services. An environmental scan of competing grocery stores has shown these services in place at their locations, and you want to know if your customers would like to have the same or similar services.

With that problem and purpose as guides, you will analyze all data (characteristics of customers, demographic data, and survey results) in terms of what they contribute to identifying which, if any, of the proposed services should be implemented. The analysis must move toward a conclusion and recommendation that will contribute to achieving the stated purpose—even if you conclude that no new services should be offered. You may recommend that the company conduct further analyses and delay decisions until more data are obtained.

Maintain a Critical Mindset

Maintaining a critical mindset requires that you constantly evaluate your data and your interpretation of the data. For example, a young, low-income management intern doing research for the grocery store might feel the need to have Wi-Fi available at the store. Knowing that, the intern should ask and answer all the following questions.

- Have I used valid sources?
- Have I gathered enough data?
- Have I gathered the right kinds of data?
- Have I permitted my biases to affect the interpretation of the data?
- Will others agree with my interpretation? If so, why? If not, why not?

One way to maintain a critical viewpoint is to discuss your research with others who are authorized to review the data, particularly during the data analysis. It is natural to develop some proprietary tendencies after working on a project for a while. You may become reluctant to discard data that are inadequate or irrelevant or to change tentative conclusions that are contradicted by the data. Individuals who have no vested interest in the project will be able to look at the data objectively and help you maintain your capacity to criticize your own work.

Apply Logical Thinking

Both qualitative and quantitative data must be interpreted logically. You can improve the quality of your analysis by understanding two basic styles of logic: induction and deduction.

As you likely know, *induction* involves reasoning from specific facts, examples, or cases to generalizations based on those specifics. Assume that in our grocery store example you look at specific data about population, family income, number of individuals in the household, and distance from the store. Based on those specific data, you generalize that the current customers and the competitive environment are favorable for more services. That is inductive reasoning. When using induction, you must be especially careful to avoid fallacies, especially these two fallacies: *hasty generalization* (reasoning that something true in one case is true in all cases) and *non-sequitur* (generalization based on inadequate data).

In *deduction*, you reason from general concepts or principles to specific facts or cases. Deduction is based on the *logical syllogism*, which has three parts:

- Major premise—a large assumption or primary fact
- Minor premise—a small assumption or secondary fact
- Conclusion—a logically inescapable inference based on the premises

In deductive reasoning, the major premise is broader than the minor premise, the minor premise is broader than the conclusion, and a detail is inferred from the more general premises. When using deduction, you must always test the accuracy of your premises, as demonstrated in the following statements:

- If either the major or the minor premise is false, the conclusion is false.
- If both the major and minor premises are true, the conclusion is valid.

In addition to using accurate induction and deduction, you can sometimes improve the accuracy of your analysis by subjecting all or some of the data to statistical analysis.

Understand Basic Analytical Procedures

Analysis of data will most likely fall into one of two types: statistical or nonstatistical. Statistics are the tools by which meaning is extracted from quantitative data. Through statistical computations, for example, you could determine average household income for an area, numbers of new homes constructed, rates of increase in both those variables, and relationships between the two. Those kinds of calculations will yield information that is more meaningful than the isolated facts represented by the raw data.

Nonstatistical analysis, often applied to qualitative data, consists of classifying or categorizing information and drawing conclusions from the review of how the data then appear. Most business research employs both nonstatistical and statistical analysis.

Nonstatistical Analysis

Nonstatistical analysis is the application of logical thought processes to extract meaning from the data. Traditionally, qualitative data were typically analyzed in that way only; but today qualitative and quantitative methods complement one another. For example, observations of communication behaviors in a group task can be observed, classified, coded, and converted to numeric values. Quantitative data also require a certain amount of nonstatistical analysis. Classification, analysis, and synthesis are three major nonstatistical methods.

Classification

As you have already seen in the discussion of data coding, *classification* is a form of data analysis whereby you assign data to categories based on established criteria. In Figure 2.1 data set, we classified income level as 1, 2, 3, or 4, depending on which category of income respondents self-identified. That classification allows for more analysis on income level when compared to other categories of data from the survey. For another example, assume that you are conducting research at a college where you teach a course each semester. You want to know whether the general characteristics of the students enrolled in your course have changed during the past 10 years. You could examine enrollments for year X and year Y and classify each student by gender, age, work experience, and marital status. You could then compare the students in year X with the students in year Y on those characteristics and ultimately draw conclusions about whether the general composition of students taking your course has changed.

You also classify data when you take notes from secondary sources and group them by subject. In the study of students taking your course, you may also want to identify new student services that could benefit those students. As you read about student services in secondary sources, you could classify your data by such subjects as services for married students, for mature students, for part-time students, and so on. Collecting data from secondary sources is the focus of Chapter 3.

For some data, classification may be the only form of analysis you perform. But often classification is a preliminary step that facilitates further analysis of the data. For example, after classifying the responses of grocery store customers (Figure 2.1) by gender, you could also determine whether males and females differ in their attitudes toward specific products or services.

Analysis and Synthesis

Analysis and synthesis require the application of deduction and induction. In *analysis*, you break a large body of information into smaller elements for scrutiny and interpretation. Imagine a gourmet who orders an unfamiliar entrée from a restaurant menu and attempts to determine the ingredients while eating the food. That person is engaging in analysis—breaking the whole into parts to discover new information. Similarly, a business researcher who looks at response data from a customer survey breaks the mass of data into parts to identify specific opinions or attitudes.

In *synthesis* you bring together individual facts and assimilate them into a broader finding or conclusion. The gourmet who attempts to duplicate at home the delicacy enjoyed in the restaurant brings together ingredients to synthesize a new recipe. Similarly, assume you have gathered secondary data—published reports—about the desirability of certain services. You study the facts reported by individual grocery stores that have attempted to initiate these services and summarize the overall success of such initiatives. The process of pulling together information reported by different individuals in various ways and summarizing that information is a synthesis process.

For most nonquantitative data, logical classification, analysis, and synthesis are the limits of data analysis. Nonetheless, those forms of analysis are critical to successful data interpretation. For quantitative data, statistical processing may also be used to enhance logical analysis and synthesis. Statistics do not replace logic; they complement it.

Statistical Analysis

Statistics is a branch of mathematics dealing with the analysis, interpretation, and presentation of numerical data. Statistical procedures range from relatively simple computations used to describe a data set to complex calculations used to analyze relationships between and among sets of data or to predict behaviors and events. The primary purpose of this discussion of statistics is to help you recognize possible statistical applications for your research. After choosing a potentially useful application, you should consult a business statistics text, such as *Statistics for Business and Economics*,[1] or a statistician for specific formulas and interpretations of results.

To comprehend any discussion of statistics, you must understand the relationship of measurement scales to statistical analysis. Such an understanding will help you select appropriate descriptive or inferential statistical applications for your data analysis.

Measurement Scales and Statistical Analysis

As noted in Chapter 1, a measurement scale is a device used to assign numbers to an element or characteristic that is being analyzed. The type of measurement scale—nominal, ordinal, interval, or ratio—determines what kinds of statistics can be used for data analysis.

In terms of power, nominal scales are least powerful; and ratio scales are most powerful. Any statistic that can be computed from less powerfully scaled data can also be computed on more powerfully scaled data. Conversely, many statistics that can be computed on more powerfully scaled data cannot be used for less powerfully scaled data. Consequently, many of the more powerful statistics can be computed only for data measured by an interval or ratio scale.

Descriptive and Inferential Statistics

Two types of statistics will be helpful here:

- *Descriptive statistics* paint a picture of the collected data. Typically, descriptive statistics include such numbers as the average or mean, the median, the mode, and a standard deviation.
- *Inferential statistics* allow researchers to make inferences and generalize results of the analysis to the whole of the population being studied.

Descriptive Stats

Descriptive statistics provide two types of information: measures of central tendency and dispersion. *Measures of central tendency* examine how the data are clustered. If you collected income data from Our Grocery Store customers, you have a specific income number for each person; thus, you can easily compute the central tendencies. The *mean* is the arithmetic average, computed by adding the reported incomes of all respondents and dividing by the number of respondents. The *median* is the midpoint of the data; half of your respondents have incomes above that point, and half have incomes below that point. The *mode* is the most frequently occurring value; more respondents report that income figure than any other figure.

Measures of dispersion show how the data are scattered around a particular point. Although your data may show that the mean income of your respondents is US$50,000 per year, you may need to know what differences exist among your subjects.

The *range* gives a concise statement of differences, showing the distance between the highest and the lowest values. Computing the range may dramatize the fact that assumptions made about an "average" customer may be quite inaccurate with respect to many of your respondents. The following example helps to demonstrate the importance of computing the range.

Annual Household Income	
$300,000	
$60,000	
$39,000	Mean income = $90,000
$30,000	Median income = $39,000
$21,000	Range = $279,000 ($300,000 minus $21,000)

In this example, if we have exactly one of each level of income, no income falls near the mean. In this case, the "average" salary, or mean, of US$90,000 is misleading because you have one customer with an outlier salary compared to others'. The *mode* tells us which value from among all values is most commonly reported. In this case, with each value appearing only once in the distribution of incomes, there is no mode as all values are represented by the same number of occurrences, in this case exactly once.

The *variance* shows the average distance between the mean and the individual values. The variance is computed using these four steps.

1. Determine the difference between the mean and each value.
2. Compute the square of each of those differences.

3. Find the sum of all squared differences.
4. Divide that sum by the number of observations.

Because the deviations are squared, the variance is expressed in "square points," a relatively meaningless number to most people. To convert the variance into a meaningful number, you take the square root of the variance. That figure, the *standard deviation*, is a measure of dispersion expressed in the same units as the original data. (*Note:* Most worksheet software, such as Microsoft Excel, can compute not only the mean, median, and range but also variance and standard deviation.)

Standard deviation is a helpful statistic if the population has a normal distribution. *Standardized normal curve*, shown in Figure 2.2, is a theoretical distribution of sample means.

The standardized normal curve has these characteristics:

- The highest point of the curve represents the mean of the distribution.
- The curve is symmetrical about its mean.
- The curve has an infinite number of cases; thus, it is a continuous distribution.

If samples are drawn from a normally distributed population, then the following statements will be true, as shown in Figure 2.2.

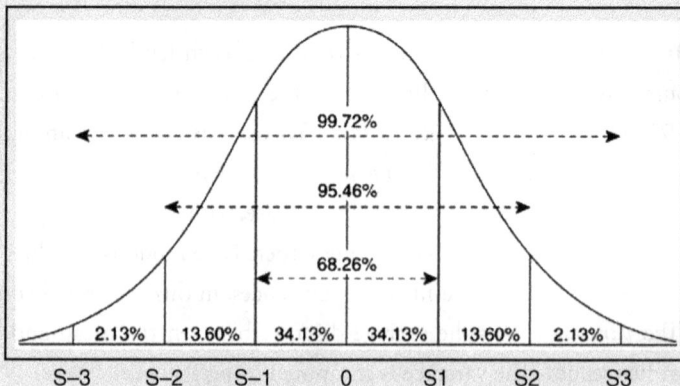

Figure 2.2 Standardized normal curve

Source: Properties of the Normal Distribution.
Note: The letter S represents the standard deviation of a sample.

- 99.7% of the observations will fall within plus or minus 3 standard deviations of the mean
- 95.5% will fall within plus or minus 2 standard deviations
- 68% will fall within plus or minus 1 standard deviation.

If your sample is normal in this sense, you have done an excellent job of selecting the sample and should have good statistics about the sample.

The concepts of the normal curve and standard deviation are essential in selecting statistical procedures and interpreting their results. A branch of statistics called *parametric* (based on fixed parameters) assumes that the population from which a sample is drawn is normally distributed. The *nonparametric* branch of statistics does not assume a normal distribution. Therefore, before selecting a statistical procedure, you must know whether the procedure assumes a normal distribution. If you cannot make that assumption about your data, then you must use a nonparametric statistical procedure.

Inferential Stats

When using *inferential statistics*, researchers make generalizations or forecasts about the population after analyzing data from a sample of that population. Inferential statistics permit you to estimate the degree of confidence that you can have in your inferences and forecasts. Results of analysis with inferential statistics are always interpreted in terms of *level of significance*, which is an estimate of the probability that the results observed in your sample are due to chance. A .05 significance level, for example, says that there is a 5% probability that your findings are chance findings and that what you observe in your sample is not typical of the population from which it was drawn. The better the significance level— that is, the lower its value as a percentage—the more confident you can be in your statistical findings.

Statistical Analysis Software

Spreadsheet and statistical software can help you prepare reports containing financial and statistical information. Conventional spreadsheets can be used to summarize data, make projections, or prepare data for complex calculations. Spreadsheets can also be used to create tables and, in some cases, figures or graphs representing the data. Those visuals can then be imported into a report that is prepared in a word-processing program.

Most statistical programs are integrated with spreadsheet or database software, permitting direct transfer of data from the spreadsheet or database into the statistical program. Commonly used programs include *Statistical Package for the Social Sciences* (SPSS), *SAS*, and *SYSTAT*. We will examine possible helpful calculations from spreadsheets and *SPSS*, using the data set described in Figure 2.1.

In this data set, we have collected information from a number of customers over a week's time. We asked for the gender, age, number of persons in the household, household income, whether the customer lives within 10 miles of the store, the average amount spent at the store in a week, and the customer's interest on a scale of 1 to 5 in potential new services. Using a typical spreadsheet software, we were quickly able to edit and code the data for simple analysis. We found, for instance, that the average score for the new service of home delivery was 3.96 on a scale of 1 to 5. We found, also, that the average score for the desirability of a senior discount was 3.90, while the desire for quick lunch was 2.04.

To further examine the data collected, you may wish to begin determining whether there is a basis for home delivery. You might reasonably assume that those of a certain age or those with a higher household income would be interested. Or, perhaps, larger families might take advantage of this potential service. With the data collected from the survey, we can perform a simple *correlation* analysis using a statistical package such as *SPSS* or *SYSTAT*. Since we have our data in appropriate form—ratio scale (simply called "scale" in SPSS) as opposed to nominal scale—we can use correlation to help us answer this question. When the correlation is performed between the values for the number in household and the desire for online shopping, we receive the following numeric values:

Pearson correlation: 0.626
Significance: 0.01

A correlation of 0.626 is a moderate-to-strong indication that those with large households would like to see home delivery. The higher the correlation (it will hit a maximum of 1.00), the stronger the correlation. The significance of 0.01 indicates that there is only a 1% chance that the correlation is due to chance.

Further, you attempt to correlate the values of the number of people in the household with income. The following values are obtained from this calculation:

Pearson correlation: 0.926
Significance: 0.01

That result (0.926) is an exceptionally strong correlation value; along with the significance value of 0.01, these results indicate an area that needs further investigation.

Note: While the purpose of this chapter is to give you the ideas of how to approach data analysis, it is not intended to be a treatise on statistics. Please refer to any standard social science statistics book for more information on statistical research methods. Examples include *Introduction to Social Statistics*[2]; *Primer on Non-Parametric Analysis, Volumes 1 and 2*[3]; *Reasoning with Statistics: How to Read Quantitative Research*[4]; and *Using IBM SPSS Statistics for Research Methods and Social Science Statistics.*[5] For a more active approach, consider one or more Massive Open Online Courses (MOOCs) in statistics, after reviewing a list of current courses available (see the MOOC List at www.mooc-list.com).

By applying logic and statistics to raw data, you should be able to state what the data show; then draw conclusions and propose action.

Three Interpretation Levels

In each stage of data reduction, you move further from the objectivity of the raw data and interject the subjectivity that inevitably accompanies data interpretation. When reporting the results of your analysis, you should carefully differentiate the levels of analysis: findings, conclusions, and recommendations.

Findings

Findings are what the data reveal. As you analyze your raw data by statistical or nonstatistical methods, you find out certain things. Findings emerge because of data interpretation.

As you present your findings in a report, follow these guides:

- Classify or summarize data; present such classifications or summaries in tables, charts, or graphs whenever appropriate.
- Interpret the data; don't merely repeat the raw data or the summary figures shown in visuals.
- Show similarities and differences among groups of data. If differences exist, supply possible explanations for those differences.

To review, you asked a sample of Our Grocery Store customers to rate the importance of five new services, using this rating scale.

1 = Very unimportant
2 = Unimportant
3 = Neutral
4 = Important
5 = Very important

Then you classified the data by tallying the survey participants' ratings for each service. Doing so showed you the percentage of participants rating a specific service in a particular way as well as the average rating for each service. Thus, your research report may include findings like those in Figure 2.3.

These findings, along with *all* others gained from the study, should permit you to draw conclusions.

6

From participants' ratings for each service, the average rating for each of the five services was calculated, as shown in Table 1.

Table 1	
Average Rating of Proposed New Services	
Service	**Average Rating**
Online shopping	3.38
Quick lunch	2.04
Wi-Fi	3.55
Senior discount	3.90
Home delivery	3.96

Source: Primary.

The average ratings in Table 1 indicate strong customer interest in new services that allow our senior customers to save money and that home delivery is important. In contrast, customers have low interest in a quick-lunch option.

Figure 2.3 Partial findings in a research report

Conclusions

Conclusions are logical inferences based on the findings. As you draw conclusions, you are moving further from the objectivity of the data and relying on your perceptions of what the data mean. To avoid unwarranted subjectivity in conclusions and to state them effectively, follow these guides.

- Conclusions must not be a mere restatement of the findings.
- Conclusions must be objective and flow logically from the analysis. If the data contradict anticipated outcomes, you must put aside your expectations and base conclusions on the available data.
- Conclusions must be relevant to the stated problem and purpose of the report.
- Conclusions must not introduce new material. All relevant data and analysis must be presented before a conclusion can be drawn.
- Several findings may be used to support a single conclusion. You need not draw a conclusion from each major finding. On the other hand, one major finding may lead to more than one conclusion.

The following examples contrast inappropriate and appropriate conclusions related to the survey of Our Grocery Store customer preferences.

Inappropriate Conclusions

> *Restatement of findings:* Customers rated services providing discounts on purchases higher than eliminating fees for seldom-used services.
>
> *Not justified by findings:* Customers will not respond to reduced fees for seldom-used services. *The survey did not mention fees for services.*
>
> *Not related to the research problem:* Our Grocery Store can gain a competitive edge by offering a variety of price-reduction strategies. *This conclusion is not justified if the stated problem is to determine customer preferences for new services and no data were gathered to determine their inclinations to choose a supermarket on the basis of the availability of those services.*

Appropriate Conclusion

> *Justified by findings, not merely a restatement of findings, related to research problem:* Customers are more interested in home delivery than in ways to save money on their grocery purchases. Our Grocery Store can satisfy some of the desires of current customers by offering senior discounts on purchases. *The matter of whether or not the store can offer home delivery is not yet known. The survey did not ask if customers would pay a fee for this service; therefore, it cannot yet be determined if this service should be implemented.*

Since research is problem oriented, you are usually expected to carry your analysis one step further—to recommend one or more solutions to the problem.

Recommendations

Recommendations are confident statements of proposed actions based on the conclusions. Recommendations must be context relevant; that is, they must respond to the purpose of the study and be appropriate for the specific audience.

As you write recommendations, observe the following guides.
- Verify that specific conclusions and findings justify each recommendation. Some report writers number summary statements of findings and conclusions so that they can refer easily to such supporting information when they write recommendations.
- State recommendations in imperative sentence structure. Begin each with an action verb.
- State recommendations specifically, including a recommended plan for implementation, if appropriate.
- Suggest additional research to investigate unanswered questions that became evident during the study.

Since the purpose of Our Grocery Store's survey was to increase customer satisfaction and loyalty by providing desired services, the following example shows an appropriate way to state your recommendations:

To increase customer satisfaction and loyalty, Our Grocery Store should initiate one new services as soon as possible and determine the feasibility of a second. Specifically, Our Grocery Store should:

1. Give a senior discount. This recommendation can be implemented by:
   - Calculating the most cost-effective way to provide the discount, such as 2% on purchases over $20, 3% discount 1 day each week, or a combination of discount methods.
   - Programming point-of-sale registers to compute the discount on total orders when a customer presents proof of senior status.
   - Training checkout associates to highlight the savings on each receipt and point it out to the customer.
2. Investigate the feasibility of home delivery. Specific facts needed include:
   - All costs associated with home delivery service
   - Radius within which deliveries can be made

By applying both logic and statistics, you should be able to interpret your data; then, reach defensible conclusions and recommendations.

Acknowledgment of Primary Data Sources

After obtaining data from and about research participants, the researcher analyzes the data and reports the results of the analysis. In that report, the researcher has a continuing obligation to guarantee the right to privacy and to protect the participants from injury to reputation, from reprisals by report readers, and so on. Those protections are usually accomplished by maintaining confidentiality—not identifying data sources unless authorized to do so.

When a researcher accepts the moral obligation to maintain confidentiality, questions may arise about the appropriate ways to acknowledge primary data sources. The following information will help you deal with that complex ethical issue.

Confidential Sources

When confidentiality has been promised to participants, primary data sources can be acknowledged only in a general way. However, confidential sources should still be recognized in the report body and in the source list. In the report body, provide a general description of the data collection method. In the source list, give a brief description of the data collection facts. The following examples illustrate accepted techniques:

Report Body

Data about Our Grocery Store's customers' demographics and opinions about potential new services to be offered were obtained by in-store surveys. Questionnaires were provided to customers with the request that they complete the survey and return it to the customer service desk. The researcher processed the data. No personally identifying information was collected and respondents were assured of confidentiality.

Source List

Customer surveys collected in store during the third week of May 2018.

Identified Sources

When subjects grant permission to be identified, source acknowledgments are similar to those used for secondary data and should be recognized in both the report body and the source list. Essential facts include *who, what, where,* and *when.* In the report body, use the same techniques that you use to cite secondary data sources (internal citation, endnote, or footnote). The following examples show acceptable ways to record interviews, observations, and surveys in a list of sources.

Interviews: *Name of interviewee* in an interview with *name of interviewer* at *place* on *date.*

Observations: Observations of *describe people, activities* at *place* on *date.*

Surveys: Survey of *describe subjects* conducted *state applicable details of method, place, date.*

Summary

The process of data analysis falls into two main categories: nonstatistical and statistical. Historically, qualitative data were analyzed with nonstatistical means. However, in recent times, methods have been developed to convert qualitative data to quantitative. Then, the statistical analysis can be used to derive meaning from the data.

When preparing for data analysis, use the following checklist to track the process.

❑ Collect the data as described in Chapter 1.
❑ Clean and code the data.
❑ Aggregate and summarize the data.
❑ Inspect the aggregated data logically for findings.

❑ Analyze the data with statistical and nonstatistical means, as appropriate.

❑ Review the analysis for additional findings.

❑ Apply logical thought to those findings and draw conclusions.

❑ In keeping with your conclusions, make recommendations for action.

CHAPTER 3

Collecting Secondary Research Data

The value of all research depends on the validity and reliability of the data acquired for the project. The acronym GIGO (garbage in, garbage out) is used often by systems analysts to remind themselves and system users to protect the quality of data that enter the system. That acronym is also an appropriate warning to business report writers and. The quality of any report can be no better than the quality of the data on which it is based. Therefore, report writers and presenters must master the skills of selecting appropriate data sources and using those sources accurately.

Choosing Suitable Types of Data

As noted in Chapter 1, your research question, divided into appropriate elements or factors of analysis, must direct your search for data. After you have defined the research problem clearly and have narrowed the scope, you must focus your attention on finding data directly related to those factors.

Data Need

Keeping the scope of analysis in mind will make you an efficient and effective researcher. You will be efficient because you will target your data search toward the sources most likely to yield meaningful information rather than wasting time looking at unrelated data. You will be effective because you will be able to judge all data in terms of its relevance to the research problem and will not be tempted to include interesting but irrelevant data.

The chart in Figure 3.1 shows how the research problem and purpose guide the selection of information sources.

Research Problem: To project market conditions for skilled construction labor in the Northwest United States during the next 3 years.

Research Purpose: To ensure that Air Waves has an adequate supply of labor to fulfill installation contracts.

Elements (Scope of the Research)	Data Needed	Potential Sources
Projected demand for skilled heating, ventilation, and air conditioning (HVAC) technicians	a. Sizes of projects under contract by major regional contractors	a. Regional contractors
	b. Projects to be bid and contracted for during next 3 years	b. State economic development boards
Projected supply of skilled technicians	a. Demographics of crews currently hired by major HVAC contractors in the Northwest	a. Regional HVAC contractors; state employment services
	b. Projected graduates from technical schools in the Northwest for next 3 years	b. Technical school registrars and placement officers; online databases such as Peterson's College Data.
Air Waves recruitment and employment practices	a. Methods currently used to locate skilled HVAC technicians	a. Air Waves director of human resources
	b. Air Waves employment practices that attract technicians to Air Waves	b. Members of current Air Waves crews
	c. Air Waves employment practices that deter technicians from working for Air Waves	c. Former Air Waves technicians

Figure 3.1 Data need determines sources

After the research problem and purpose have been defined, the scope of analysis must be narrowed. Then specific kinds of data and specific data sources must be identified for each element in the scope. Note in Figure 3.1 that more than one kind of data and more than one data source may be required to analyze a specific element adequately.

Secondary versus Primary and Tertiary Sources

Effective business researchers use both primary and secondary data to solve business problems. You are already familiar with primary data—facts acquired at their sources through experiments, interviews, observations, questionnaires, and company records.

Secondary data consist of information that others have accumulated and made available through books, journals, magazines, websites, and other publications. (*Note:* A *journal* is a scholarly periodical reporting original research on a single topic, including a references list, and published by an academic or association press. A *magazine* is a periodical covering multiple practical topics in one issue, with few or no references, published by a commercial publisher.)

Tertiary data are found in sources that combine material from secondary sources. Examples include blogs, *Encyclopedia Britannica*, many textbooks, and Wikipedia. Tertiary sources can be very helpful for background research, before your research problem is firmly stated. However, these sources—meant for a general audience—tend to oversimplify the research they present. Therefore, try to find the original material that is summarized in a tertiary source.[1]

Some researchers mistakenly consider primary data to be better than secondary data. They assume that information "straight from the source" is better than secondhand data. Others prefer to use primary data because they are stimulated by that data collection process and feel restricted when they must sit at a computer or in a library searching for secondary data.

In contrast, some researchers—also incorrectly—suspect the accuracy of primary data. They recognize that people can deliberately distort self-reported information, and researchers can make incorrect observations or lead people to report what the researcher wants to record. In addition, some researchers may feel uncomfortable with the primary data collection process but enjoy the sense of discovery that comes from searching out well-documented information in secondary sources. Neither attitude can produce consistently effective research reports.

When you recognize a problem and the need for research, consult secondary sources first. Secondary sources often provide information to help define the problem more clearly and to identify elements that should be studied. Then, after narrowing the scope of the analysis, you can determine whether primary or secondary sources will best answer each element of the problem, as demonstrated in Figure 3.1. When the problem you are investigating is unique to your organization, primary data may be the only usable information. But if adequate secondary data are available, you should use those data instead of spending the time and effort required to use primary sources effectively. Problems like yours probably have occurred in other organizations or have been researched by others, and the solutions may be reported in business publications. Although these problems will differ slightly from your own, your knowledge of what other individuals and organizations concluded in similar situations can help to answer your questions.

Collecting secondary data includes (1) locating the data, (2) evaluating the data source, (3) extracting the data from its source, and (4) keeping data records. Case 3.1 outlines the research process when secondary data are used. Notice that the research steps are essentially the same as those discussed in Chapters 1 and 2 (primary data).

Case 3.1

Collecting and Using Secondary Data

You surveyed students at a college where you teach a course each semester. You determined whether general characteristics of students enrolled in your course had changed in the past 10 years. You examined enrollments for 2007 and 2017 and classified each student by gender, age, work experience, and marital status. You then compared the students in 2007 with the students in 2017 on those characteristics. Based on the results of statistical analysis, you concluded that the general composition of students taking your course has changed. While the ratio of men to women is practically the same, your 2017 students differed from their 2007 counterparts in age, work experience, and marital status. Specifically, your survey produced these findings.

- Current students are younger by 4.25 years than students 10 years ago.
- Based on age, today's students belong to Generation Z, while students in your class 10 years ago were solidly in Generation Y.
- The 2017 students came to your class with 21.6 months less work experience and less business-related experience than your 2008 students.
- Of your 2017 students, 21% were married; of your 2008 students, the proportion of married students was 16.7%.

Upon learning of your research, the college dean asked you to conduct another study. What implications do student differences have for the student services offered by the college and the instructional methods you and others use?

1. Is it logical to think that instructional methods should change because today's students are 4 years younger?
2. What do you know about differences between Generation Y and Generation Z? Do you suppose those differences are important relative to student services or instructional methods?
3. What services are typically offered for married students? What is the trend in this area?

Mentally, you review steps in the research process, asking yourself questions and then answering them.

- *What type data will I need?* Experience tells me to start with data from secondary sources. Once the research problem and purpose are absolutely clear, I'll come back to this question.
- *How should I collect secondary data?* I must track down and evaluate a variety of relevant sources—websites; higher education journals and magazines; possibly reference books; maybe one or more proprietary databases, such as ERIC (Education Resources Information Center). I'll need to read widely and record any information that specifically addresses the research problem, once it's been defined.
- *How can I classify and analyze secondary data?* When I identify and then record the key information in each source—that's the beginning of my data analysis. Classifying the data will involve sorting my many notes cards (data records) by subject. And analysis will continue as I synthesize the information from my notes.
- *Will I need to draw conclusions and make recommendations?* Of course. Once I synthesize the data, I'll use logic to interpret what those findings mean. Then I'll reduce them to plausible conclusions. And from my conclusions, I'll recommend important, practical changes in student services and instruction.

This chapter is meant to help business researchers locate, evaluate, and extract secondary data and maintain data records. First, though, consider the tools needed for completing these four steps economically and well.

Preparing Vital Research Tools

Whenever your data needs include secondary sources, acquire or cultivate these research practices for maximum efficiency during the data collection process.

- Become familiar with a style guide for recording secondary sources (references) and citing these sources in a research report.
- Review your techniques for searching the web and find ways to upgrade those procedures.
- Become acquainted with more than a few general search engines for searching the visible web as well as deep-search engines designed for the invisible web. For collecting data across social media networks, become acquainted with several social media search engines.
- Know how to evaluate secondary sources, especially online sources.
- Skim available data sources and create an annotated list of the sources that appear to offer the richest data. Then return to the most promising items on that list.
- Become skilled at recording and classifying secondary data, using both verbatim and paraphrased records.

With these tools in place, you will be equipped to collect secondary data efficiently and effectively.

Become Familiar with APA or Other Style Guide

A *style guide* is a set of standards for writing and formatting documents, ranging from academic journal articles to internal business reports. Some style guides are for general use—for example, White and Strunk's *The Elements of Style*.[2] Other guides may be meant for a specific publication, organization, or field. APA style, for example, was created for the American Psychological Association (APA). However, this style is widely used in other behavioral and social sciences, including, government, education, and business. APA style is shown in *Publication Manual of the American Psychological Association.*[3] Other frequently used guides include:

- *AP Style Book*[4] used largely by magazine publishers, marketing departments, and public relations firms
- *Bluebook*[5] used mainly by members of the legal profession
- *Chicago Manual of Style*[6] used primarily by authors and publishers of books and journals in the humanities and some science fields
- *MLA Handbook*[7] used mostly by writers in the humanities and literary fields

Most style guides, including these four, are available online, usually in abbreviated form. Some online versions may involve a subscription fee.

The purpose of any style guide is to improve communication through consistency and the application of best practices in language usage. In this book, Chapters 3 and 4 emphasize two uses of APA style: citing secondary sources in business report text and listing all such sources in the report's References section—the last page(s) of the report body. *Note:* Most organizations that routinely produce research reports require the use of just one style guide. Therefore, when joining a new organization, determine which of the many style options is the preferred one.

Review Search Techniques for WWW

You are likely good at generating keywords and entering them in your web browser to search for needed information. Perhaps you have also experienced frustration when your search results are less than expected or too numerous. See Figure 3.2; adding one or more of these techniques to your repertoire may save search time and boost your effectiveness.[8]

Get Acquainted with General, Deep-Search, and Social Media Engines

As a long-time Internet user, you are likely so familiar with the Google *search engine* that you use its name as a synonym for the verb *search*. You may also use other members of the Big Four: Bing, Yahoo, and Ask.[9]

Use this search technique	How-to information	For this reason
At the outset of a research project, search using wild card characters: asterisk (*), pound sign (#), and question mark (?).	In the search field, type a root word followed by a wild card character. Example: print*	Broadens your search; results will include other forms of the word. Example: printable, printed, printer, printing, printing industry, printing services, printmaking, printmaker, printout, prints, and so on.
Search with more than one search engine.	Choose multiple engines from the various types listed in this chapter.	Ensures a thorough search, as no two engines return identical results and some engines focus on one kind of results, such as books or forums.
Search for a specific phrase rather than a single keyword.	Type quotation marks before and after the phrase in the search field. Example: "printed newsletter ideas"	Tells the search engine to return only results containing the phrase—all words and in the order you typed them.
In most search engines, use Boolean commands AND (or +) and NOT (or -) to regulate your search. Note: The OR command is the search engine default; the NEAR command is equivalent to using quotation marks around a phrase.	In the search field, type keywords with AND or + between them. Example: newsletter+printed Alternatively, type keywords with NOT or – between them. Example: newsletter-email	Returns results including the words newsletter and printed. (Includes printed newsletters.) Returns results including the word newsletter but excluding the word email. (Omits email newsletters.)
Search only for websites that contain your keyword in the web address.*	In the search field, type inurl: and your keyword. Example: inurl:newsletter	May yield additional sites that are narrowly focused on your research topic.
Search only a specific top-level domain, such as.com,.edu,.info,.net, or.org.**	In the input field, type site: and the domain extension and your keyword or phrase. Example: site:.org "printed newsletter ideas"	Narrows your search to a specific, top-level area of the web.
Search for a keyword (or phrase) on a web page.	With the web page open, press CTRL+F. In the pop-up input field, type the word you are seeking.*	Saves you time and tedium during an extensive web search.
Search a website with a search engine rather than the site's built-in search tool.*	In the input field, type site: and the URL of the site to be searched and your keyword or phrase. Example: site:companynewsletters.com "printed newsletter ideas"	Makes your searches faster and more accurate than built-in search tools.

Once your research problem and purpose are set, search very specifically.	In the search field, type a phrase including all qualifiers. Example: "newsletter printing services in Harrisburg, Pennsylvania"	Returns only specified results.

*Technique tested in Bing (Microsoft Edge browser), Google (Google Chrome browser), and Yahoo (Firefox browser).
**See a complete list of domain name extensions at Quackit (www.quackit.com).

Figure 3.2 Web-search techniques

To plan for data collection for business reports, you can benefit from other search utilities, including portals and vortals, meta-search engines, search aggregators, and deep-search engines.

General Search Engines

You have likely heard of a search engine referred to as a "spider" that crawls around the web seeking websites. The spider reads the found websites, as it were, and arranges all or part of the text on them into a large index or database that you, the user, can access. No search engine covers more than about 30% of the Internet, though some of them—especially the Big Four—are huge.

Some popular, but smaller, search engines include Boardreader (boardreader.com), BuzzSumo (buzzsumo.com), CC Search (search.creativecommons.org), CrunchBase (www.crunchbase.com/#/home/index), and DuckDuckGo (duckduckgo.com).[10]

Some engines are called *web portals* because they provide not only search capabilities but also a point of entry to a range of web services, such as e-mail, news, social media, stock market quotations, popular videos, and weather. Google and Yahoo are web portals, along with Data.gov (catalog.data.gov/dataset) and MSN (www.msn.com). The main idea is to provide one web page for users that combines a broad range of content from many other systems or servers. These broad-range sites are also called *horizontal portals* to distinguish them from portals focused on a specific audience or industry.

Infoplease (www.infoplease.com) is a horizontal portal, providing access to almanacs, atlases, biographies, dictionaries, and encyclopedias along with national and world news and other services. Atlases feature maps and detailed profiles of the world's 193 countries and the 50 U.S. states. Current encyclopedias cover the main branches of knowledge (communication, engineering, logic, mathematics, natural sciences, philosophy, and social sciences). In the areas of business and finance, Infoplease provides statistics and facts about United States business and commerce, including foreign trade and the stock market; consumer resources, including agencies and organizations, fraud, guarantees and warranties, patents, product safety, recalls, and trademarks; economy, including federal budget, health insurance, income, labor and employment, and poverty; personal finance, including saving for college, stock market investing, and retirement planning; and the tax system including the Internal Revenue Service, federal and state taxes, and filing information.

A *vertical portal* or *vortal* is a portal for a niche audience, such as a specific age group, alternative lifestyle, community, ethnic group, gender, interest, religion, industry, or market. For example, someone who enjoys DIY (do-it-yourself) projects might visit the Kreg Tool Company's vortal, buildsomething.com; guru.com is a vortal for independent professionals; and www.uruguay.com provides information about Uruguay (hotels, maps, news, locations, pictures, restaurants, and so on).

Industry-specific vortals usually provide discussions, news and newsletters, online tools, research and statistics, and other services to inform users about a certain industry. Examples include Gartner Research (www.gartner.com/technology/research.jsp), a vertical portal for technology professionals; Contractor (www.contractor.com), a vertical site for the construction industry; and The Vortal (www.thevortal.com / main), a site devoted to fostering and training consumer electronics professionals. Women in CE (thevortal.com/women-in-ce) is a vortal that caters to women in the consumer electronics industry.[11] The following vortals are particularly relevant to business people.

- *Business.com* (www.business.com), a human-edited web directory, consists of in-depth information in seven business areas: entrepreneurship, finance, human resources, marketing, office management, sales, and technology. The vortal also includes a blog (www.business.com/blog) and a tool for obtaining price quotes on background checks, call centers, copiers, credit card processing, direct mail, GPS fleet-tracking software, payroll, phone systems, point-of-sale systems, security, small business loans, and web design.

- *FindLaw* (www.findlaw.com) covers a range of legal areas, including consumer protection, employment law, immigration law, product liability, real estate law, small business law, state laws, and tax laws. In addition, FindLaw includes question-and-answer forums on legal issues; guidance in choosing the appropriate form in a legal situation; a tool for creating such forms for individuals and businesses; news articles involving legal issues; and access to a wide variety of legal blogs.
- *globalEDGE*™ (globaledge.msu.edu), a vortal for international business professionals and created by the International Business Center (IBC) at Michigan State University, connects its users around the world to information and resources on global business activities. The Global Insights section offers international business and trade information for more than 200 countries and all U.S. states. It also covers over 20 industry sectors and many of the world's trade blocs. The Reference Desk section provides an expert-reviewed directory of resources, including cultural and economic information, trade law and trade tutorials, and statistical data.
- *SinglePoint* by Northern Light (www.singlepointportal.com), a gateway for business researchers, provides employees of large organizations access to and analysis of business news, social media content, and primary and licensed secondary research.[12] The range of accessible knowledge includes basic company information; business documents; competition details; e-books; financial analyst research; government databases and websites; IBM Connections sites; industry news feeds; IT analyst research; business journals; and market data, research, analysis, and strategy. Almost any research that a company creates or licenses also can be integrated into SinglePoint.

Meta-search Engines

A *meta-search engine* is one that sends your keywords to several other search engines and delivers a combined list of the search results. Meta-search, also known as *federated search*, is based on the premise that the web is too vast for any one search engine to index all of it and that more complete search results can be found by merging results from multiple engines. In this regard, Google and Yahoo qualify as meta-search engines.

Unlike general engines, a meta-search engine lacks a database. Instead, it creates a virtual database by taking your search request, sending it to several diverse engines, and then compiling hits based on the engine's unique set of rules.

Each meta-search engine is different. Some search only popular search engines; others combine lesser-known engines and other sources. These engines also differ in the number of search engines they use and how they present search results, as noted in the following list of meta-search examples.[13]

- *iboogie* (iboogie.com) lists many related search terms on your SRP (search results page), speeding up your searches.
- *Search* (www.search.com) is a popular choice due to simple operation and familiar appearance; its SRPs look like Google search results.
- *Turbo Scout* (turboscout.com) is a large, data-rich mega-search engine.
- *Unabot* (www.unabot.com/meta.shtml) gives you a vast collection of mega-search engines. It also allows you to refine your search by country.
- *Vroosh* (www.vroosh.com) lets you choose a worldwide version or a version for the country you are researching.
- *Yippy (*www.yippy.com*)* permits you to specify a domain, website, or file type for your search, providing focused results for your data needs.

Search Aggregators

A *search aggregator* is a meta-search engine that finds, filters, and sorts results into categories, using RSS (rich site summary) technology. An advantage of search aggregators is flexibility in deciding which engines will fill your research needs. Generally, an aggregator allows you to select the engines for a specific search. The following meta-search engines operate as aggregators.

- *Dogpile* (www.dogpile.com) gives you search results from a variety of the biggest, most popular search engines. You can request a general web search or ask to see hits sorted into one or all of five categories: images, news, videos, white pages, and yellow pages.

- *Mamma* (www.mamma.com) is a search aggregator that enables you to search the web, or specify one or all of four categories: suggested articles, images, news, and local content. Mamma uses your location information to provide local search results that are on target. It involves a tab view—each category of hits on a separate tab.
- *WebCrawler* (www.webcrawler.com) combines results from the Big Four and searches the web for images, videos, news, or white pages.

Deep-Search Engines

The *visible web* is that part of web content that standard search and meta-search engines can find and index. Other names for it are Indexable Web and Surface Web. Most of the web's content, however, is buried in the *invisible web*, far down on pages that do not exist until a specific query generates them. Conventional search engines cannot find this information, called *dynamic content*. Other information below the surface includes:

- Web pages that no other page links to
- Text written in a format other than HTML
- Text content using protocols other than HTTP
- Sites that require users to register and log in, including many searchable databases
- Sites that block search engines
- Ever-changing content, such as news and stock market reports

Besides invisible web, common names for these seemingly unreachable sites—vastly more numerous than the surface web—include Deep Web, Deep Net, Hidden Web, and Undernet.

A deep-search engine is designed to search the invisible or hidden web that regular engines cannot reach. (Deep-search engines return hits from both the visible and invisible web.) The search results may include a list of web addresses along with the characteristics of each source found. Therein lies the main deep-search challenge: how to find and map similar data from many, dissimilar sources and then present an understandable list of results.

Deep-search engines are extremely powerful mega-search engines. Some of that power derives from links to many, many databases as well as the ability to search dynamic content. The following list identifies a few deep-search engines for locating business information.[14]

- *BizNar* (biznar.com/biznar/desktop/en/search.html), a deep-web business research portal, searches approximately 70 authoritative business sources simultaneously. Then before results are presented to the user, duplicates are removed and the list is ordered according to a relevance ranking algorithm. BizNar searches a wide variety of resources, including government sources, news, periodicals, and social networks.[15]

- *DeepDyve* (www.deepdyve.com) provides access to millions of articles from thousands of journals in 26 subject areas, including business, management, and accounting; computer science; decision sciences; economics, econometrics, and finance; energy; environmental sciences; psychology; and social sciences. DeepDyve indexes every word in an article and (using artificial intelligence) looks at the meaning of an article and uses that information to compute a relevance statistic. This statistic is an index of the article's relevance to your search terms. In 2017, DeepDyve involved a $40 monthly subscription, with a 2-week trial available at no charge.

- *Infomine* (www.infomine.com) searches, or mines, information from articles, bulletin boards, databases, directories of researchers, electronic books and journals, mailing lists, online library card catalogs, and other resources. Nine subject areas include business and economics and government information.

- *Library Spot* (www.libraryspot.com), a vast engine providing access to a variety of online libraries (academic, film, government, law, medical, national, presidential, public, and state); reference tools (almanacs, calculators, calendars, dictionaries, directories, encyclopedias, genealogy, grammar and style, historical documents, how-to information, maps, public records, quotations, statistics, telephone directories, thesauruses, time data, and ZIP codes); and periodicals (books, headlines, magazines, and newspapers). The reference tools include a business directory to many well-known databases, such as BizWeb, Edgar Online, Hoovers Online, and Thomas Register. These databases are described later in this chapter.

- *The WWW Virtual Library* (http//vlib.org) roughly maps the World Wide Web and delivers data sources in 16 broad categories, including business and economics, computing and computer science, international affairs, regional studies, social and behavioral sciences, and society. (The Virtual Library is one of several examples of human-edited *web directories* that are listed here as search engines. While directories and search engines are different technologically, both serve the purpose of helping users find data on the Internet.)

A small part of the deep web is known as the *dark web* and cannot be accessed by any of these search engines. While some dark web communities want to conceal illicit activities, such as buying and selling illegal drugs, human trafficking, pornography, and terrorism, other user groups are simply anti-establishment or pro-privacy and want to operate without anyone watching. Legitimate uses of the dark web include making anonymous reports of domestic abuse, government oppression, and other crimes that have serious consequences for the so-called whistle blowers. Access to the dark web is controlled by requiring specific proxying software that hides users' IP (Internet protocol) addresses, plus several additional layers of verification.[16]

Social Media Search Engines[17]

Social media represents a relatively recent source of secondary data for business research. Many businesses now track daily on one or more social media platforms (Facebook, Flickr, Google+, Instagram, Pinterest, Tumblr, Twitter, Vimeo, YouTube, and others) for both historical (past week or two) and real-time data about that organization's brand (product or service) performance on social media. The primary purpose of such tracking is to engage with social media users when appropriate (answer questions or clear up confusion, for instance) and reply when necessary (for example, respond quickly and professionally to negative messages or opinions). Most social media data are analyzed and turned into improvements—such as shorter posts or brighter colors for images—designed to bring new visitors and new customers to the company's website.

Some of the data are qualitative: what people around the world are saying about the business, the current trends across one or all social media platforms, what influencers (authors, bloggers, journalists, presenters, and so on) are saying about the brand, and the popular keywords displayed at a specific social media site.

Other social media data are quantitative: demographics (location, language, and gender of people who comment to the company's social media posts), engagement (number of interactions people have with the posts, such as comments, likes, retweets, and shares), impressions (number of times the content is displayed), reach (number of people who see the posts), sentiment (positive-to-negative ratio of comments), and strength (how often the brand is discussed).

Most social media platforms have their own search capability, such as Facebook Advanced Search, Pinterest's Guided Search, Twitter Search, and YouTube FastSearch. The independent search engines are usually superior in depth and speed of searches and the ability to analyze and summarize collected data. Their capacity for searching multiple social media platforms in one place is the biggest advantage of independent search engines. The following list describes a few of the newest and most popular social media engines.

- *IceRocket Tracker* (www.icerocket.com). IceRocket's Big Buzz feature allows you to search Facebook and Twitter posts, plus blogs, images, news, and the web—all from one page in real time. This search engine involves filter options for tailoring the search results. For instance, you can search for a certain blogger's posts or sort tweets by hashtags.
- *SmashFuse* (www.smashfuse.com). Trending keywords are displayed on the homepage of this free social media search engine, which covers many platforms (or the one you specify): Facebook, Flickr, Google Plus, Instagram, Pinterest, Tumblr, Twitter, Vimeo, and YouTube. Real-time results are presented in small parcels along

with helpful images; thus, you can easily choose the results you consider most relevant.

- *Social Mention* (www.socialmention.com). This free option presents real-time search results visually, focusing on the passion of postings (how likely a person will repeat a mention) as well as strength, sentiment, and reach. Additionally, you can request an RSS feed of your brand's mentions and identify the hashtags, keywords, and user names appearing most often.

- *Social Searcher* (www.social-searcher.com). This engine allows you to search social networks in real-time and yields deep analytics data. You can search without logging in for publicly posted information on Dailymotion, Facebook, Flickr, Google+, Instagram, Reddit, Tumblr, Twitter, Vimeo, and YouTube. In addition, you can save your social mentions history and set up e-mail alerts to be notified when content you specify appears on a social media network. Filters enable you to narrow your search results by sentiment, post type, and social media platform. Basic, standard, and professional subscription plans are available, along with a free 14-day trial.

- *Talkwalker Alerts* (www.talkwalker.com/alerts/login). This search engine gives you brand mentions over the past seven days across Instagram, Twitter, and YouTube, plus blogs, forums, and news. (To include Facebook results in your search, just connect your Facebook account to Talkwalker.) You can search by country and media type. Data collected include demographics, engagement levels, influencers' names (websites as well as social media), sentiment analysis, and themes in word-cloud form (a visual representation of text, with the frequency or importance of each word shown by font size or color). Additionally, a world map shows where brand mentions originate; and pie charts show the sentiment in each country. The vendor offers basic, corporate, and enterprise pricing plans.

Generally, use multiple search engines to locate secondary sources. Start with one of the basic engines. As you learn more about your research problem and the topics (keywords) involved, use a meta-search engine. When an aggressive search is required, call on one or more deep-search engines.

Along with the ability to search and find secondary sources goes responsibility for evaluating them.

Increase Your Awareness of Evaluation Criteria

A researcher must evaluate source reliability and continue to search for data until satisfied that, within the time and budget constraints of the research project, the most valid and reliable sources have been found. The following checklist will help you evaluate the reliability of all secondary sources:

- *Timeliness:* Is the source current? If outdated, the source should not be used.
- *Relevance:* Does the source address the research problem? Even if extremely interesting and timely, sources should be used only if they address the problem specifically.
- *Accuracy:* Is the source reliable and unbiased? Is the author a recognized expert? Did the author use a reliable data collection method? Where and how were any statistics derived? Does the source include complete information? If any answer is no or doubtful, the source should not be used.
- *Quality:* Is the information verifiable, consistent, and properly referenced? What discrepancies do you expect? For example, while expert opinions may differ, data discrepancies might result from differences in geography, population, or company size.
- *Cost:* Will the available data lead to an appropriate, cost-effective solution to the problem? If primary data would lead to a better solution, the data collection cost may be justifiable as opposed to using the lower-cost secondary data.

Evaluate sources on the web extra carefully since that information constantly changes; website sponsors do not often employ fact-checkers as print publishers do; and many websites serve sponsors' commercial interests. In addition, consider that many websites do not reveal who authored the content or what his or her qualifications are for writing on the topic. Rarely does a site include information for contacting the author. Almost anyone can publish on the Internet. In addition, many websites do not link to credible outside sources.

Blogger McCartney Taylor emphasized the importance of vetting authors when evaluating secondary sources. In addition, Taylor devised a scorecard for screening authors.[18] Each article begins with a score of 5; then bonuses are added or penalties subtracted as follows.

+6   Author is recognized for publishing in refereed journals.
(A *refereed journal* contains articles written by topic experts and reviewed by several other experts in the field before the article is published in that journal. Another term with identical meaning is *peer-reviewed journal*. Usually, reviewers of an article do not know who its author is. Thus, the article succeeds or fails on its own merit, not the reputation of its author.[19])

+5   Work contains references to primary sources (+2 for secondary references). Taylor recommends checking on a few of the cited sources. If even one is false, pointless, or irrelevant, subtract eight (−8).

+3   Article appears on an education (.edu) or government (.gov) website.

+2   Article is published by a trustworthy news medium, such as *Los Angeles Times, The New York Times, The Wall Street Journal,* or *The Washington Post.*

+2   Author publishes articles in popular (not peer-reviewed) journals.

+2   Author provides a USPS address.

+1   Author provides an e-mail address.

−1   Article uses *they* vaguely to represent influential, powerful people in the field but nowhere identifies the individuals or group by name.

−2   Article appears on a free web hosting site—such as bluehost, eHost, or iPage—or a free blog—such as Ghost, Medium, or Jekyll.

−4   Article appears with no author named (no penalty for unattributed government or police reports).

−4   Article is disorganized and contains grammatical or spelling errors or both.

Taylor provided these guides for interpreting total scores on his scorecard: When the total is 0 to 3, ignore the source; when, 15 or more, the source is likely believable. For scores of 4 to 7, be cautious though this author may be somewhat credible. For scores of 8 to 14, you can likely trust this author's credibility.

While blogs show the date and even the time of posting, many websites exclude both the origination date and when the site was updated. Another time-related problem: Even a relatively up-to-date site may include dead links; that is, links to sites that no longer exist or that are woefully outdated.

These qualities of the Internet make it necessary to redouble your efforts when evaluating a web-based data source. Since the Internet's inception, various organizations—ranging from Consumer Union[20] to university libraries[21]—have set guidelines for website evaluation. Some of the early evaluation instruments included eight or more question categories and up to 20 narrow questions in each group. Today, most evaluation checklists include three to five question categories, comparable to the evaluation checklist in Figure 3.3. Use of this form is recommended until its questions become embedded in your memory.

Generate a List of Likely Sources in Advance

Before you start recording and then classifying secondary data, explore a range of possible sources and create an annotated bibliography, a descriptive list of potential electronic and print sources. A *bibliography*, as you likely know, is a list of journal articles, blogs, books, websites, and so on related to your research problem and purpose. The list includes details about each item—such as the author, title, publisher, web address, and database name if applicable. An *annotation*, a paragraph around 150 words, accompanies each bibliography entry as shown in Figure 3.4. This abbreviated example represents research into the potential payback of a company newsletter and a comparison of digital versus printed news-letters. Specifically, the research problem is to identify typical benefits and costs of e-mail and printed newsletters used for direct marketing by retail organizations. The research purpose is to conclude whether an

Web Source Evaluation Checklist		
Directions: If unsure of an answer while visiting a site, check No. Likelihood of a trustworthy site increases with each Yes answer.		
	Yes	No
Authority and Identity		
• Does anyone claim to be author (not same as webmaster) of the site?		
• Are the author's credentials shown?		
• Is the author's employment affiliation included?		
• Do you recognize the author's name as someone qualified to write on this topic?		
• Does the page include information for contacting the author?		
Objectivity		
• Is the author's aim clear? Is the aim to inform (rather than entertain, earn a profit, or persuade)?		
• Does the site present different viewpoints and/or discuss the options open to you?		
• Is the emphasized viewpoint reasoned (rather than based on emotion)?		
• If the site is sponsored by an organization, is that organization a known, reputable one?		
• Does the text contain a minimum of words (adjectives and adverbs) suggesting how you should feel about the topic?		
Accuracy and Quality		
• Is the information detailed and thorough (rather than sketchy or shallow)?		
• Does the information square with your knowledge and experience?		
• Can you find the same information points in two other places?		
• But does the site offer "something different" or "something more" than other sources?		
• Does the author support and explain statistics? For example, do research results describe data sources and sample selection procedure and size?		
Currency		
• Does the page show the date it was posted or updated?		
• Was the page posted or updated recently enough for your research?		
Coverage and Navigation		
• Is the site complete (no pages under construction)?		
• Can you find a list of references/sources?		
• Do all the links to other websites work?		
• Is the site easy to navigate (with minimal clicking and scrolling)?		
• Do you have any reservations about the site in question?		

Figure 3.3 Evaluation form for web sources

Source: Kuiper and Clippinger (2013).

Annotated Bibliography

N Beard. (2014, February). Print newsletters as content marketing tactic: Pros, cons, examples and best practices. [Web log post]. Retrieved from http://www.toprankblog.com/2014/02/print-newsletters-content-marketing-tactic

> This blog post cites a 2014 B2C and B2B content marketing report. Both groups of marketers use print newsletters to meet marketing goals. Lists six research-based reasons why print newsletters work. Also, lists print newsletters' pros and cons. Shows three polished examples and comments on each one. Provides a thorough list of guidelines for content marketing with a print newsletter. Links to related posts. Very rich source.

D Kandler. (2012, October 2). Tips to make your company newsletter more cost effective [Web log post]. Retrieved from http://www.companynewsletters.com/costeffect.htm

> This blog post focuses on payback, printing, and mailing. It cites ways to make company newsletters fill their purpose and indicates ways to control printing and mailing costs. An insightful article.

D Kandler. (2013, July 23). How to avoid the most-common company newsletter mistakes [Web log post]. Retrieved from http://companynewsletters.com/mistakes.htm

> This blog post identifies seven common mistakes and includes a thorough discussion of each one. The author uses rich examples and demonstrations. Links to related posts.

Buck, S. (2013). *Newsletter marketing: Insider secrets to using newsletters to increase profits, get more new customers, and keep customers longer than you ever thought possible.* North Charleston, SC: CreateSpace Independent Publishing Platform.

> This book discusses the importance of newsletters to an organization's bottom line—successful marketing, client retention, business growth. It also contains a trove of how-to information. The author, Shaun Buck, is viewed as an expert on company newsletters.

Jarvinen, J., Tollinen, A., Karzaluoto, H., & Jayawardhena, C. (2012). Digital and social media marketing usage in B2B industrial section. *Marketing Management Journal, 22*(2). 102-117.

> This journal article focuses on B2B digital marketing. It cites barriers, practices, and usage of direct marketing by digital means, including e-mail newsletters. The study revealed that B2B firms were not fully using the digital media available. Provides a line of reasoning for using digital newsletters, though its focus is broader.

Neely, A. (2016, August). Rare.us wrangles success with email campaign. *DMN (Direct Marketing News)*. Retrieved from http://www.dmnews.com/marketing-strategy/rareus-wrangles-success-with-email-campaign/article/518824

> This online magazine article explains how one business used e-mail newsletters to increase its website views to 400 million. Brief article includes content marketing strategies.

Figure 3.4 Annotated bibliography (in APA references style)

e-mailed newsletter or printed newsletter sent by USPS would be more cost effective for Our Grocery Store.

The annotation contains your description and evaluation of the bibliography item. Annotations are helpful reminders of how you rated the relevance, accuracy, and quality of each potential source. Incidentally, if you prepare a bibliography using BibMe, popular citation management software, the program lets you insert annotations along with the bibliography entries. Citation management software is discussed in Chapter 4. This publishing information enables you to return to the item if you choose, read it closely, and record specific data directly related to the problem and scope of your research. *Note:* If you locate a source by using a deep-web search engine (discussed later in the chapter), *capture its data immediately*, along with the publishing information. The reason is simple: A later deep-web search may omit the source. Likewise, if you locate a printed source in a library's collection, record the data and the publishing information at the same time. In both situations, include the source in your annotated bibliography.

Arranging the potential sources by type, rather than alphabetically, facilitates data collection. In Figure 3.4, for example, blogs are listed first, then a book, followed by a journal article and magazine article. When you find a data source—especially a journal article or book—check for references to other possible sources. The list of references near the back of a book or at the end of a journal article may include additional sources you can add to your bibliography.[22] In creating an annotated bibliography, for the sake of efficiency, follow a style guide—either the APA style demonstrated in Chapter 4 or the style manual preferred in your organization.

While creating an annotated bibliography, you will cover a lot of ground quickly; thus, you may be led to redefine or tweak your statement of the research problem even before you finish the list. Later, when preparing your research report, your annotated bibliography will be a draft of the references list. To revise the references list, make the changes in this checklist.

- Decide if the references list in your report will include annotations. If readers are unlikely to benefit from annotations, delete every one.
- Delete any publication that you did not cite in your report's findings. A references list contains only cited sources.
- Arrange the references in alphabetical order.
- Insert any cited publications (and annotations) not already on your list.
- Replace the Annotated Bibliography heading with the word References (when using APA style).

Though similar in appearance, a bibliography and references list involve format and style differences. More importantly, a bibliography—rarely used in business reports—would contain cited sources as well as sources that influenced your thinking but are not cited in your report.

Be Adept at Recording Secondary Data

Once you find relevant information, you must extract it from its source for use in your data analysis and report. Thus, you will need skills and tools for recording *verbatim* (word for word, exactly as written) data and *paraphrased* (translated into your wording) data and a means of tracking sources. Creating an annotated bibliography as recommended earlier in the chapter, gives you a head start on tracking.

Verbatim Data (Quotations)

Record information verbatim when you must preserve the exact nature of the data. For example, when you attribute a controversial statement to an individual, it is wise to quote the statement exactly as it was written or spoken. Similarly, when reporting certain statistics, the exact numbers, even to two or three decimal places, may be significant in your research.

Two commonly used techniques for recording secondary data verbatim are note taking and copying.

Note taking involves capturing exact information from the source onto an actual or virtual note card. As you know, people internalize information through the five senses: sight, hearing, taste, smell, and touch. For most individuals one of these senses is dominant or preferred, and for about 65% of us that is sight (visual mode). However, in roughly 5% of us the sense of touch (tactile mode) is strongest. For these individuals, especially, handwriting data on lined 3 × 5, 4 × 6, or 5 × 8 cards comes naturally. Conversely, you may prefer to use a notes program such as Evernote (www .evernote.com) or the OneNote component of Microsoft Office, which is available for online use at www.onenote.com. Another online option is SuperNotecard (www.supernotecard.com). In addition, sticky note apps are plentiful on the web. Figure 3.5 shows a virtual note card containing verbatim data and a separate note card showing the data source.

Both cards in Figure 3.5 were created in a free app named Notezilla (www.notezilla.en.softonic.com). Features of Notezilla and similar apps allow you to sort your virtual note cards into separate memoboards (folders). In addition, you can assign a tag (a keyword or topic in your research report) to each note card; and then, sort the notes by those tags.

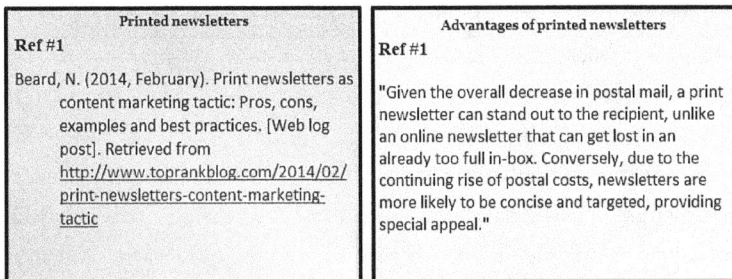

Printed newsletters	Advantages of printed newsletters
Ref #1	**Ref #1**
Beard, N. (2014, February). Print newsletters as content marketing tactic: Pros, cons, examples and best practices. [Web log post]. Retrieved from http://www.toprankblog.com/2014/02/print-newsletters-content-marketing-tactic	"Given the overall decrease in postal mail, a print newsletter can stand out to the recipient, unlike an online newsletter that can get lost in an already too full in-box. Conversely, due to the continuing rise of postal costs, newsletters are more likely to be concise and targeted, providing special appeal."

Figure 3.5 Note cards showing data source and verbatim data

To use the note-taking technique, follow these guides.

- If you created an annotated bibliography, number each listed source. Otherwise, prepare a reference card for each source you consult. *Note:* If multiple colors are available, use one note color just for references. Follow your style guide to arrange complete who, what, where, and when information. Number each reference card as you prepare it.
- Use a separate card for each quotation. *Note:* Choose one note color to use only for quotations.
- Write the number of the source above the quotation.
- Copy material exactly as it appears in your source. Check for and correct even minor typing errors.
- Place quotation marks before and after the material to remind you that the material is directly quoted.
- When using a printed source, write the page number(s) on which the quotation appears. This step will help you relocate the source if needed when preparing your research report.
- Before leaving a cited source, verify the accuracy and legibility of each quotation, paraphrase, and reference. Such editing ensures accuracy and saves time by eliminating the need to return to a source yet again for verification.

For some people copying printed pages or printing web content is a convenient alternative to note-taking. When copying material from a printed publication or printing content from a website, immediately prepare a reference note card OR record the reference information on the copy or printout itself, as shown in Figure 3.6.

Although some verbatim data may be appropriate in a business report, excessive use of such data tends to suggest that the report writer lacks the ability to analyze and synthesize information. Therefore, you must become proficient at paraphrasing data.

Figure 3.6 Blog printout with handwritten reference

CompanyNewsletters.com 2017. Used by permission.

Reworded Data (Paraphrases)

When you write a paraphrase, you capture the essence of the information by summarizing key facts and stating them in a way that is relevant to your analysis. Paraphrased data are more desirable than exact quotations when the basic meaning is important but specific wording is not. For example, if you are reporting a company's growth for a 3-year period, it may be more meaningful to compute and report a percentage of increase in gross revenues for each year than to report the exact gross revenues. Computing and recording percentages of increase based on exact revenues that you find in a secondary source is a form of paraphrasing.

Even when information is paraphrased, you must cite your data source. Therefore, you should record sources and extracted, paraphrased text like the note cards kept for verbatim data—omitting the quotation marks from the recorded data. The data note card should contain a subject heading, the number of the related source, and, for printed sources, the page number of the original data from which you wrote your paraphrase (see Figure 3.7).

Printed newsletters	Printed newsletters: Considerations
Ref #3 Kandler, D. (2013, July 23). How to avoid the most-common company newsletter mistakes [Web log post]. Retrieved from http://companynewsletters.com/mistakes.htm	According to Kandler (2013), an erratic distribution schedule for printed newsletters is the most egregious mistake companies make. If the newsletter's nameplate indicates a quarterly edition, the four issues should be evenly spaced throughout a calendar year. A related mistake: failing to allow adequate editorial time to plan and prepare each issue. Allow *seven hours for each page* (8.5x11), Kandler advised. Then multiply by the number of pages in your company newsletter and add hours for designing, proofing, and correcting.

Figure 3.7 Note card showing data source and paraphrased data

Following these 10 steps will help you paraphrase another writer's ideas in an ethical manner.[23]

1. First, read the material to understand it. Do not write until you get the information you need; then hide the source.
2. Write your note card without looking at the source. Cover up the printed page or minimize the computer screen.
3. Do not copy and paste text directly from a website into your report draft. It is too easy to think of the copied text as yours once it is in your report.
4. Notify readers at the beginning of a sentence that someone else originated the following text. Examples:
   - In a 2014 blog post, Beard reported that print newsletters continue to hold value as a content marketing tactic.
   - At CompanyNewsletters.com, Kandler introduced the concept of a hybrid, or two-in-one, newsletter.
   - According to Bear, a printed newsletter should include jump lines and end signs to help readers navigate the pages.
5. Write the idea in your own words. Imagine presenting the idea to a coworker or friend; then write the words you would use in that situation.
6. Use only that part of the material needed to make the point you want to convey. Also, write a concise summary rather than including details from the source.

7. When finished recording your paraphrase, compare it to the source. Be sure you did not use the same words or phrases or simply rearrange or replace a word here and there.

8. If you have reason to use *more than a six-word string* from the source, put quotation marks around those words, turning them into a direct quotation within your paraphrase.

9. Compare your text and the original again to ensure that your facts are accurate and that you preserved the meaning of the source.

10. At the end of your paraphrased text, remember to show where the idea came from.

Locating Secondary Sources

Many secondary business data sources can be accessed on the web without using a search engine. Additionally, though online data services continually expand, be prepared to use a library's print sources, microforms, and database subscriptions to collect secondary data.

World Wide Web

The long list of secondary sources on the Internet is divided into four categories; namely, business and industry directories, digital libraries, country profiles, and online databases. Most listed sources may be accessed free of charge; the exceptions are noted.

Business and Industry Directories

Directories help you find data about companies and industries in and outside the U.S. A brief description of each directory follows its title in the following list.

- *Agency ComPile* (www.agencycompile.com). Directory of marketing communications agencies. Offers searchable database of advertising, public relations, direct marketing, sales promotion, and related fields.

- *Agency Search Directory* (www.aaaagencysearch.com). Find advertising agencies by demographics (location, service type, size, and so on), keyword, or name (agency, management, client or brands). Compiled by 4A (American Association of Advertising Agencies).
- *Alibaba* (www.alibaba.com). International marketplace of businesses looking for businesses (customers, partners, suppliers) and products.
- *AnnualReports* (www.annualreports.com). Access 53.000 annual reports from 5,100 companies worldwide, using seven search criteria: alphabetically, company name, exchange, index, industry, sector, or ticker symbol. View reports in HTML or PDF formats and order a hardcopy (if available).
- *BizWeb Directory* (www.bizwebdirectory.com). Lists 46,000 business and shopping websites in 200 categories. Provides company and product information.
- *Corporate Affiliations*™ (http://corporateaffiliations.com/default /index?id= routetohome). Search nearly 2 million company profiles and over 3 million decision-makers. Shows corporate hierarchies, including parent company and related subsidiaries. Subscribers can sign up for company-specific business news feeds and e-mail alerts when an executive moves from one company to another. Involves a subscription, with a seven-day free trial.
- *Corporate Information* (www.corporateinformation.com). Offers analytical reports on 39,000 companies from 85 countries. Includes quality ratings for many companies. Reports contain explanatory footnotes to help interpret company results. Two subscription plans available.
- *Kompass* (http://us.kompass.com). Search for business tools and solutions across 5 million selected company profiles in more than 60 countries in this business-to-business (B2B) site.
- *OneSource Company Research* (https://custom.onesource.com /company-research.aspx). Provides company profiles based on relevant news, key executives, regulatory filings and corporate family structure, and revenue and growth patterns.
- *Public Register Online, The* (www.annualreportservice.com). View or request hard copy of 5,000 online annual reports or 10-K presentations (yearly report required by U.S. Securities and Exchange Commission

[SEC], giving comprehensive summary of companies' financial performance). Very like The Public Register (www.publicregister.com).

- *ThomasNet®* (formerly Thomas Register). B2B buyers and engineers can search 700,000 industrial suppliers in 17 business categories to discover those with matching business goals. Suppliers can upload ads at this site. Includes news, a blog, and many related services.
- *WallStreet Research™* (www.wallstreetresearch.org). Find corporate profiles, newsletters, and detailed research reports on emerging small-cap (roughly, market capitalization between $300 million and $2 billion) companies.

Digital Libraries

Valuable secondary sources include wide-ranging electronic publications—from articles, blogs, and books to recordings, trade magazines, and videos. The following list names and describes collections of such content.

In general, the following *digital library* examples could also be called *complete-text databases*. That is, the library contains the complete contents of books, dissertations, journals, magazines, newspapers, and other written documents.

- *BPubs* (www.bpubs.com). Collection of business publications and articles from widely varied sources (for example, e-zines, consulting companies, and government agencies). All listed publications are available free of charge.
- *CEO Express* (www.ceoexpress.com/home). Comprehensive source of business information in four broad categories: daily news, business research, tools and travel, and break time. Involves a nominal membership fee.
- *Factiva* (www.factiva.com) by Dow Jones. Provides over 36,000 global news sources, including blogs, images, licensed publications, influential websites, and videos. Most of the top sources are not available on free web. Includes a Publisher Portal. Involves a subscription.
- *FindArticles.com* (www.findarticles.com). Search CBS network news and technology sites for articles on any topic. Contains 500 periodicals dating to 1998.

- *HighBeam Research* (www.highbeam.com). Search full-text articles in thousands of academic journals, encyclopedias, magazines, newspapers, newswires, and trade magazines. Involves a subscription.
- *JSTOR* (www.jstor.org). The Register and Read component provides free access to individuals. Open an account; search for an article; and read a preview. Adding an article to your reading shelf—up to three at a time—enables you to read full text. After 2 weeks, articles can be replaced by three new ones, for a total of 78 free articles a year. (JSTOR also operates as a proprietary database, as noted on page 000).
- *Library of Congress* (www.loc.gov). World's largest library contains millions of books, newspapers, manuscripts, maps, photographs, and recordings. Research arm of U.S. Congress and home of U.S. Copyright Office.
- *PsycARTICLES* (www.apa.org/index.aspx). Contains full-text, refereed articles on psychology and human behavior from 117 journals published by American Psychological Association. Includes some historical content dating to 1894. Involves a modest membership fee; the website describes membership options and fees. *Note:* A proprietary database ProQuest (see page 000) encompasses the PsycARTICLES library.

Country Profiles

The business community is a global one. Business in the 21st century requires extensive knowledge—culture and customs, economic background, history, politics, and risk factors, to name a few—of countries or world regions outside your own. Compilations of such data are invaluable to decision-makers in international business. The following list shows names and locations of country profiles.

- *CIA World Factbook* (www.cia.gov/library/publications/the-world-factbook). Find information about 267 world entities (communications, economy, geography, government, history, military, people, transnational issues, and transportation. Includes many maps.
- *Country Indicators for Foreign Policy, or CIFP* (www4.carleton.ca/cifp). Research-based statistical tables of foreign policies and conflict risk countries, including roughly 40 countries deemed fragile.

- *FreeLunch* (www.economy.com/freelunch/default.asp). Download economic and financial data from 180 countries, 150 metropolitan areas worldwide, and all U.S. states, metro areas, and counties. Provided by Moody's Analytics.

- *Geospatial One Stop, or GOS* (www.sciencebase.gov). Collection of geographic data including metadata records (information about the data) and links to live maps, downloadable data sets, and more.

- *International Data Base, or IDB* (www.census.gov/population/international/ data/idb/informationGateway.php). Offers demographic indicators for countries and areas of the world with population of 5,000 or more. Funded by the Census Bureau's International Programs.

- *U.S. Foreign Trade Highlights* (www.census.gov/foreign-trade /statistics/ highlights/index.html). Includes top trading partners, monthly international trade report summary, and monthly and annual press highlights. Also, includes links to other foreign trade topics and statistics generated by the U.S. Department of Commerce.

- *World Bank Open Data* (http://data.worldbank.org). Find global development data and statistics for developing countries. Browse by country or 20 economic indicators.

- *World DataBank* (http://databank.worldbank.org/data/home .aspx). Specialty statistical indicators for 264 countries. Country data ranges from gross national income (GNI) to the percentage of the population who use the Internet.

Online Databases

Other collections of secondary data accessible from the Internet, *online databases*, are plentiful, as the following list attests. The list includes *commercial databases* as well as government-sponsored and other databases. Descriptions highlight the distinctive features of each database.

- *AlphaSense* (www.alpha-sense.com). Database for equity investors (investment managers, global banks, research firms, and corporations). Key data on more than 35,000 international businesses.

- *American FactFinder* (https://factfinder.census.gov). Provides access to wide-ranging data about United States, Puerto Rico, and Island Areas. Data come from several censuses and surveys.
- *Bankrate.com* (www.bankrate.com). Database of interest rates for over 300 financial products. Data come from surveys of 4,800 financial institutions in all 50 U.S. states.
- *BigCharts* (http://bigcharts.marketwatch.com). Offers real-time quotes and performance charts on stocks and mutual funds traded on NASDAQ and other exchanges. Includes interactive charts, industry analysis, and market news and commentary.
- *BizFilings* (www.bizfilings.com/about.aspx). Offers guides, resources, and tools for starting and running a business. Includes comparison of business types.
- *Catalog of U.S. Government Publications, or CGP* (https://catalog.gpo.gov/F?RN=319705784). Find electronic and print publications from executive, judicial, and legislative branches of U.S. government. Includes 500,000 records and is updated daily. Provides links to online publications and a Federal Depository Library directory for print publications.
- *Electronic Data Gathering, Analysis, and Retrieval, or EDGAR, Online* (www.edgar-online.com). Offers searchable company data and public federal SEC filings for equities, mutual funds, and other publicly traded assets. Involves a subscription fee. *Note:* FreeEdgar (www.searchedgar.com) lets you search full text of all SEC documents filed in past several days.
- *Energy Information Administration, or EIA, International Energy Data and Analysis* (www.eia.gov/petroleum). Find statistics on crude oil, gasoline, diesel, propane, jet fuel, ethanol, and other liquid fuels. Includes fuel prices, crude reserves and production, refining and processing, imports and exports, stocks, and consumption and sales.
- *E-Commerce Statistics, or E-STATS* (www.census.gov/programs -surveys/e-stats.html). Devoted to measuring the electronic economy. Features background papers, information on methodology, and recent and upcoming releases.

- *FedStats* (https://fedstats.sites.usa.gov). Includes data and trends from 100 federal agencies on U.S. aviation safety, crime, economy, education, energy use, farm production, population, health care, and more.
- *U.S. Government Publishing Office, or GPO, Economic Indicators* (www .gpo.gov/fdsys/ browse/collection.action?collectionCode=ECONI). Access economic information on business activity, credit, employment, Federal finance, gross domestic product, income, international statistics, money, prices, production, and security markets from 1995 to current month. Data to 1948 available through Federal Reserve Archival System for Economic Research, or FRASER (https://fraser.stlouisfed.org).
- *Hoovers®* (www.hoovers.com). Data on 85 million corporations and 1,000 industries. Largest single source of business information. Subsidiary of Dun & Bradstreet.
- *Intelligize* (www.intelligize.com). Offers resources for the Securities and Exchange Commission, or SEC, compliance and regulatory information to corporations, law, and accounting firms. Involves a subscription.
- *Internal Revenue Service, or IRS* (www.irs.gov). A portal, or comprehensive source of income tax information—credits and deductions, filing, forms and publications, help and resources, news and events, payments, and refunds. Special section for tax professionals.
- *Kauffman Entrepreneurs* (www.entrepreneurship.org). Numerous articles and resources about developing business ideas and starting and growing a business. Involves a subscription.
- *Mergent Online™* (www.mergentonline.com/login.php). Basic subscription includes U.S. company data or international company data or both. Subscribers can choose from 14 additional modules. Includes business description, history, long-term debt and capital stock, officers and directors, property, and subsidiaries. Financial statements appear as reported and in native currencies, ensuring data integrity.
- *Mintel* (www.mintel.com). Offers consumers' opinions on each new food and drink product in the U.S. Focuses on product

attributes, such as brand, healthfulness, and taste. Includes qualitative (verbatim opinions) as well as quantitative purchase intelligence. Involves a subscription.

- *Morningstar* (www.morningstar.com). Provides data on 525,000 investment offerings and real-time, global market data on 18 million commodities, equities, futures, indexes, options, and precious metals, plus foreign exchange and Treasury markets. Operates in 27 countries. Involves basic and premium subscription plans; includes a 2-week free trial.
- *NASDAQ Trader* (www.nasdaqtrader.com). Database of stock market data, performance statistics, and trading products, plus news and resources from the NASDAQ stock exchange.
- *Office of Science and Technology Information, or OSTI* (www .osti.gov). Database of U.S. Department of Energy research and development activities. Includes huge collection of science presentation videos.
- *Quandl* (www.quandl.com). Access economic, financial, and social data sets for research. Seek new ways to predict lending risk of individuals and institutions from nonfinancial information (alternative data). Even when data are downloaded to Excel, Python, or R program, usage requires API (application program interface) key, available free at website. Includes both free and subscription data.
- *Small Business Administration, or SBA* (www.sba.gov). Articles and resources for starting and managing a small business, including loans and grants approval activity. Includes government contracting information.
- *Securities and Exchange Commission, or SEC, Info* (www.secinfo .com). Comparable to EDGAR (searchable SEC filings) database but more user-friendly.
- *Slideshare.net* (www.slideshare.net). Search for slide decks (mostly), documents, infographics, and videos. Build knowledge quickly from succinct, absorbing content by leading business professionals. Over 35 categories and 18 million uploads.
- *United States Patent and Trademark Office, or USPTO* (www .uspto.gov). Find general information about patents, intellectual

property, and trademarks and the step-by-step process to apply for and maintain a patent or trademark. Search for specific patents and trademarks.

- *Yahoo! Finance* (https://finance.yahoo.com). A portal to rich sources of stock market information. Create a watchlist of specific stocks; then access the list for real-time stock quotes. Includes customized news and alerts.

Brick-and-Mortar Libraries

The vastness of the web may lead you to conclude that you can do all your research from there. However, libraries do have several advantages not found on the web. Pause for a moment to consider those advantages, shown in Figure 3.8.[24]

Locating Data on the Web	Locating Data in a Library
Many resources are free; others require you to buy a subscription.	You have free access to practical and scholarly information, paid for by the library.
Information is not evaluated for accuracy and may be biased, distorted, or even fabricated.	Content of books and magazines (printed or in a library database) is evaluated for accuracy and authority.
Websites are ephemeral. A selected site may be taken down before you collect the needed data.	References are quite stable over time, often having long publishing histories.
The Internet is largely unorganized.	Subject pages in databases help you quickly find precisely the data you need, and reference librarians can help, too.
Search engines may return over a million hits with no quick way for you to determine relevance to your topic.	Databases let you limit or expand your search to find just the articles you need.

Figure 3.8 Comparison of locating sources on the web versus in a library

Several types of libraries serve a variety of patrons and needs, including researchers in business and many other professions. Academic, or university, libraries contain strong research collections that support faculty and student research. Often these libraries maintain robust collections in certain areas but not in others. Business, or corporate, libraries serve a specific clientele. Such libraries include those of companies, professional associations, trade associations, institutes, or research agencies. Narrow in focus, corporate libraries offer depth in their specific areas. These libraries, though usually not open to the public, offer advice and answer questions by e-mail or phone. Public (community-based) libraries, general in nature, collect information for a broad user population.

Most libraries list books and periodicals and other available items in either an online database (accessible from the web via software as service, or SaS, products) or a local database (accessible from the library's own computer or its external storage, such as a CD). Thus, users can search the catalog and produce a list of available items, along with full reference information for each item, a brief description of its contents, and where and how to access it. Most online catalogs can be searched by author, keyword, library call number, subject, or title.

Proprietary Databases

A *proprietary database* is privately owned and password protected—and usually not accessible to the public from the web. To access its contents, one must obtain rights from its owners to access the database on a local network. Typically, individual users do not obtain rights, however. Instead, academic, corporate, and public libraries pay the steep subscription fees. Then individuals gain access with a student ID, employee ID, or library card. *Note:* Users can access proprietary databases from a dedicated computer in the library. In addition, most academic and public libraries enable users to access databases from their own desktop computers or laptops.

An individual user's rights may involve certain conditions and restrictions, such as limitations or prohibitions on copying, sharing, or redistributing the material. Generally, such limits are mild and do not interfere with efficient use of the database. In comparison with online and commercial databases, the proprietary kind are more dependable for users. In addition, data stored in proprietary databases are usually protected under copyright, contract, patent, and trademark laws.[25]

Searching for sources in a proprietary database is like searching the web. Relevance of the data you get will depend largely upon your use of appropriate search terms. Also, databases allow you to place additional limits on your search results, by specifying certain features of the items you are seeking. For instance, you can indicate that you want only refereed articles available in complete text and published in the past 3 years.[26]

The following list names and describes selected proprietary databases for business researchers.

- *Business Source Complete* (formerly *Business Source Premier*). Includes all business disciplines: accounting, banking, finance, management, marketing, and others. Complete-text articles and abstracts for the most scholarly business journals, some dating to the 1880s.
- *Checkpoint.* Contains financial accounting, tax, audit, and corporate governance resources.
- *CultureGrams.* Offers concise cultural and statistical views of every country recognized by the United Nations.
- *EconLit.* Covers economics writings in books, journals, and working papers.
- *GreenFILE.* Focuses on the relationship between people and the environment.
- *IBISWorld.* Contains industry market research reports, covering each industry's statistics, structure, sensitivities (such as demographic and macroeconomic factors not controlled by companies within the industry), and success factors.
- *International Security and Counter Terrorism Reference Center.* Offers information on essentially all dimensions of national security and counterterrorism.
- *JSTOR.* Includes a wide variety of academic journals, including journals for business and related fields; books, and primary sources, including business documents. With an extensive archived journal component, the current journals collection is limited. Very few journals are less than 3 years old.
- *LexisNexis Academic.* Provides access to more than 6,000 business, legal, and news sources, including business publications; regional, national, and international newspapers; SEC filings; and trade journals to name a few.
- *MRI* (*Mediamark Reporter*). Provides data about the U.S. consumer magazine audience, measuring the readership of roughly 250 magazines.
- *Passport.* Offers business intelligence on consumer lifestyles, industries, and market data and forecasts. Also, provides analysis of the business environment, economy, and infrastructure of

177 industries in 200 countries. Source of distribution channel analysis and historic and forecasted market sizes.

- *ProQuest.* Includes e-books (nearly half a million), a huge collection of dissertations and theses, newspapers (global, national, regional and specialty papers spanning three centuries); and scholarly journals and periodicals. Ten individually titled databases include the Business Premium Collection, a largely full-text database with dissertations, market reports, newspapers, scholarly journals, trade publications, working papers, and other sources relevant to business and economics. Content is usually accessed through library Internet gateways, but this website offers a Connect page: www.proquest.com.

- *SRDS Media Solutions.* Provides data for advertising media, such as circulation, market analysis, and rates. The specific media included may not be identical for every subscriber. Subscription options include digital websites, out-of-home media, radio, and TV and cable media.

Reference Books

References books are an excellent source of historical business data. Since most are revised and republished annually, the content may be viewed as current, unless your research problem and purpose require up-to-the minute data. Using a reference book usually involves a library visit, as a single volume may cost several thousand dollars. A library's reference section typically contains general business information sources, such as books about business careers and business and social customs around the world. To locate relevant, timely reference books, you may also search a library's online catalog, using keywords from your stated research problem and the techniques you use to search the web.

The specialized reference books in the following list are generally available in huge national libraries and public libraries, especially those located in metropolitan areas. In addition, you will likely find these references in academic libraries, particularly school of business libraries; and, in corporate libraries. The list omits classic business references that continue to be published in book form but are currently available on the Internet.

- *2016 Million Dollar Directory: America's Leading Public and Private Companies* (published in five volumes). Offers extensive coverage of private and public companies, primary and secondary lines of business (up to six for each company), and names and titles of major decision-makers. Updated annually.

- *Craighead's International Business, Travel, and Relocation Guide to 90 Countries.* Contains information about business, cultural, and everyday living environments. For each country, includes overview and history and current economic and political structure. Also, includes etiquette for business meetings and entertainment and a range of concerns, such as banking and money, family life, health, housing, language, schools, and transportation, for individuals planning to live and work in one of the countries.

- *Hoover's Handbook of World Business.* Provides facts on more than 750 of the world's large, most influential companies based outside the U.S. Includes private, public, and state-owned enterprises worldwide. Organized by location of business headquarters, industry, and company executives. Includes products and services, directors of public companies, and mergers and acquisitions.

- *Political Risk Yearbook.* Includes 100 country reports in eight regional volumes—Central and South Asia, East Asia and the Pacific, East Europe, Middle East and North Africa, North and Central America, South America, Sub-Saharan Africa, and West Europe—also available separately. Current edition available online or on CD-ROM at same price as the book ($2,475).

- *Principal International Businesses.* Lists the 50,000 largest employers worldwide, located in 140 countries. Includes agriculture, autonomous government entities, communications, construction, films and other service businesses, financial institutions, fishing, forestry, insurance, manufacturing, mining, power generation and distribution, real estate, and transportation. Organized three ways: alphabetically, geographically, and by product class.

- *Standard & Poor's Register of Corporations, Directors and Executives.* Source for company identification. Indexed by executive and directors' names, geographical location, and Standard Industrial Classification Code.

- *Ward's Business Directory of U.S. Private and Public Companies.* Features 112,000 company entries, 90% of them privately held companies. Includes current and historical data. Lists company name, description, and type; codes (Standard Industrial Classification, or SIC, and

North American Industry Classification System, or NAICS); contact information (e-mail, USPS, and web addresses, FAX and phone numbers); number of employees; and operating revenue.

Business Periodicals and Periodicals Index

Journals reporting business research are a mainstay of academic and corporate libraries, as well as databases, digital libraries, and vortals, as previously noted. Scores of such journals are published online or in print or both. Some classics date from the early 1900s, and new titles emerge regularly. Obtaining an exact count of scholarly business journals is practically impossible, and listing a few examples here would be most unhelpful. One way to identify academic business journals in your chosen field by title: Search the web, using information in Figure 3.9.

Most academic and public libraries also subscribe to business magazines and newspapers, such as *Bloomberg Businessweek* and *The Wall Street Journal*. Popular business magazines often found on library

In the search field, type these words: Top business academic journals in _____, replacing the blank with a business field from the following list.				
Example: Top business academic journals in accounting				
accounting	business research	fashion marketing	manufacturing	records management
advertising	computer science	forecasting	marketing	risk management
auditing	consumer services	futures market	materials management	small business
banking	corporate communication	hospitality management	operations management	statistics
big data analysis	data mining	human resources	organizational behavior	strategic management
business communication	econometrics	infographics	organizational culture	supply chain management
business ethics	economics	information systems	production	technical writing
business law	entrepreneurship	international business	psychology	technology
business leadership	facilities management	management sciences	purchasing	tourism management

Figure 3.9 Search terms for identifying scholarly business journals

shelves include titles in the following list. Some of these titles, such as *The Economist* and *Forbes* can be accessed online. Most of the other titles include a digital edition, and you can subscribe at the publisher's web page.

- *Adweek*—Features stories on the best advertisements, as well as trends in marketing, branding, and other aspects of business.
- *Bloomberg Businessweek*—Follows up-to-date business and offers financial news, stock advice, and in-depth coverage on major businesses and business events.
- *Consumer Reports*—Known for research-based (unbiased) reviews of modern consumer products.
- *The Economist*—Covers U.S. business and economics and delves into the world economy, providing specific information on the economies of countries worldwide.
- *Entrepreneur*—Focuses on small business founders, giving advice on start-up, initial and continued management, and other aspects of running a successful company.
- *Fast Company*—Covers the latest strategies and trends in business; takes a fresh approach to entrepreneurship.
- *Forbes*—Read for updated news related to business and finance.
- *Fortune*—Covers all aspects of business news. Known for the Fortune 500, a list of the world's most powerful companies.
- *Harvard Business Review*—Contains new ideas and classic advice on innovation, leadership, and strategy from the world's best business and management experts.
- *Inc.*—Focuses on growth and improvement for entrepreneurs. Includes ways to enhance business presentation skills and profiles of successful companies.
- *TechCrunch*—Profiles tech startups and reviews new Internet products; also, offers breaking technology news.
- *Wired*—Covers wide-ranging tech topics and how advances in technology impact our lives.

Most libraries also subscribe to *Business Periodicals Index* to help you access articles in journals, magazines, newsletters, newspapers and so on by author, subject, or specific topic. *Note:* The *Index* covers articles at least one column long in roughly 500 periodicals published in the U.S.

and elsewhere. For an article you choose—whether a current one or an historical article—the index directs you to the correct periodical title, date, volume and issue, and page numbers. *Business Periodicals Index* may be available in print, in a library database, or both.

Older magazines may be bound as books, or they may be housed in the library's microform collection. *Microform* is a general term for material that contains small images of periodicals. These page images may be found on film rolls (*microfilm*) or film sheets (*microfiche*). Because the images are tiny, special scanners are used to view the pages. Of course, microforms save storage space, as thousands of periodicals can be stored in a few cabinets.

The wide range of available secondary sources requires that you be as proficient at locating data in a library as you can on the web.

Summary

Begin a research project by collecting secondary data unless your problem is unique. Once your research problem is set, you may, or may not, see a need to collect primary data, too.

Locating and evaluating secondary sources, extracting data from sources, and keeping data records will be easier for you if you are competent in these areas.

- Able to record and cite sources in line with a style guide, such as APA.
- Know a variety of techniques and shortcuts for searching the web.
- Use varied search engines in addition to Google, including deep-web engines, and know the characteristics of each one.
- Can apply criteria to evaluate the validity of secondary sources, particularly online sources.
- Know how to assemble an annotated bibliography to control and guide data collection efforts.
- Equally skilled at extracting and recording verbatim data and paraphrased data from sources.
- Use actual or virtual note cards to record and cross-reference data and sources. Also, record descriptive titles on note cards to aid data classification.

Many business data sources can be accessed on the web, using a URL rather than a keyword search. However, even the most adept web user looking for secondary business sources can expect to use library print sources, microforms, and database subscriptions, too.

Data sources on the web fall into four categories (with some overlap among them):

- Business and industry directories
- Digital libraries
- Country profiles
- Online databases

In each category, a few websites will likely become your go-to sources, saved in your browser's bookmarks or favorites. In the directories category, for example, you may find yourself going to these sources repeatedly.

- Corporate Affiliations (http://corporateaffiliations.com/default/ index?id= routetohome)
- Kompass (http://us.kompass.com)
- The Public Register Online (www.annualreportservice.com)
- ThomasNet (www.thomasnet.com)

Digital libraries may contain books, as well as journals and magazines and other publishing media. Keep these library websites at the ready.

- BPubs (www.bpubs.com)
- FindArticles.com (www.findarticles.com)
- HighBeam Research (www.highbeam.com)

International business information will be indispensable to your career. Top online sources for global business data include these websites.

- CIA World Factbook (www.cia.gov/library/publications/the-world -factbook)
- International Data Base (www.census.gov/population/international/ data/idb/informationGateway.php)
- World DataBank (http://databank.worldbank.org/data/home.aspx)

Among the numerous online databases, you will likely identify several that you go to often. Predictably your favorites will include one of more sites on this short list.

- Bankrate.com (www.bankrate.com)
- Catalog of U.S. Government Publications (https://catalog.gpo .gov/F?RN=319705784)
- EDGAR Online (www.edgar-online.com)
- GPO ECONI (economic indicators from Government. Publishing Office) (www.gpo.gov/fdsys/ browse/collection.action?collection Code=ECONI)
- Hoovers® (www.hoovers.com)
- Mergent Online™ (www.mergentonline.com/login.php)

For locating secondary sources, academic, corporate, and public libraries offer advantages not available on the web. For example, proprietary databases in libraries provide uncommon flexibility for expanding or narrowing searches. Unlike web content, essentially all library content has been evaluated for accuracy of facts and expertise of authors. Also, library references are constant over months, years, even decades, while websites come and go.

The following list includes widely used proprietary databases.

- Business Source Complete
- CultureGrams
- IBISWorld
- LexisNexis Academic
- Passport
- ProQuest

Some classic business references continue to be published in book form only. Among them are the following data-rich sources.

- *Craighead's International Business . . .*
- *Million Dollar Directory*
- *Hoover's Handbook of World Business*
- *Political Risk Yearbook*
- *Standard & Poor's Register . . .*

A publication titled *Business Periodicals Index* is an invaluable tool for locating secondary sources in a library. It is organized by author name, subject, and article title. Whether a printed or digital version of the *Index*, it will give you the details—article title, journal or magazine title, even the page number or numbers—for tracking down the articles you decide to read.

Since the quality of data in your reports determines their value, honing your ability to select appropriate data sources and use them accurately are wise moves on your part.

CHAPTER 4

Documenting Secondary Data Sources

This chapter illustrates the mechanics of acknowledging, or documenting, the sources of secondary data you use for your reports. The examples shown demonstrate the American Psychological Association's (APA's) style manual, which is available in most bookstores and online. Documenting involves two procedures:

- Creating a detailed, alphabetical list of all sources referred to in the report. The list has a one-word title, References, and is inserted into the report after the last content page.
- Citing each source briefly when referring to it in the report.

Before we delve more deeply into how to treat sources, consider Case 4.1. Though the details in the case are fictitious, the situation is one encountered frequently in the business environment.

Case 4.1

Copyright Infringement Charged

At your Clark & Childs Consulting office yesterday, you received a business letter from Primus, Johnson & Agesen, a prominent group of intellectual property lawyers in the Atlanta area. You opened the letter promptly and noticed the subject line, CEASE AND DESIST. First,

(continued)

you skimmed the letter to get the gist; then, carefully reread parts of the message to be sure of its content.

Hartsfield Press, the publisher of *Catch the Drift* (2018), an e-book authored by Thomas Wu and Jean B. Harding, claims that you infringed its copyright in your business report titled "Let's Talk Safety." Because of this claim, the letter instructs you to remove the report file from Clark & Childs's website, where it has increased traffic to the site in the past month. In addition, you are warned to discontinue selected report slides you posted at SlideShare.net following your oral presentation of "Let's Talk Safety" to a client.

You recall referring to *Catch the Drift* as a source for "Let's Talk Safety" and lifting and adapting a few of its graphs. However, you are puzzled by the suggestion that you violated the copyright. As you always do, you included in-text citations wherever you paraphrased the authors' ideas as well as where you quoted Wu and Harding's words. Also, you included a source note for each graph you recreated. In addition, as usual, you listed a complete reference for *Catch the Drift* in the report's references list. So, you wonder, what is the problem?

Before responding to the attorney's letter, consider these rhetorical questions.

1. Isn't copyright infringement the business term for what your college instructors called plagiarism? If not, how does copyright infringement differ from plagiarism?
2. Did you intentionally recreate blocks of *Catch the Drift*'s content in your report? If so, what proportion of that publication appears in your report?
3. If you do not take down your "Let's Talk Safety" report and slide deck as requested, what do you think will happen?
4. Looking beyond the current situation, what steps would be appropriate in the future to preclude a similar cease-and-desist letter?

The following discussion sheds light on the important queries in Case 4.1.

Responsible Use of Copyrighted Material

Experienced, ethical writers of business reports agree that every report creator should acknowledge his or her unique sources of information for four reasons:

- The business and academic communities expect honesty in all transactions. When you indicate where or from whom you obtained unique information, you are following standard academic and business practice.
- The business and academic communities appreciate the ability to build on previous knowledge. When you indicate where you obtained your information, you are enabling others to find the data and use it in their academic or business research.
- The business and academic communities respect individual contributions. When you *document* the sources of data that you acquired from others, including direct quotations and paraphrased material, the readers may infer that any undocumented material is your contribution to the body of work.
- Documenting sources helps a writer avoid *plagiarism*, an ethical lapse in which a person claims credit for a work he or she did not create, or uses someone else's work without proper attribution.[1]

In short, when you acknowledge your data sources you demonstrate authority and integrity as a business writer and researcher.

Plagiarism: A Closer Look

Ponder this alternative definition of plagiarism: "The intentional or unintentional failure to give credit to the originator of ideas, facts, words, and rhetorical structures that are not the writer's own."[2] This definition is notable for two reasons.

- This definition brings up the possibility of unintentional plagiarism.
- This definition indicates that text is not the only thing that can be plagiarized. *Notes:* The term rhetorical structure refers to how an idea is expressed. John F. Kennedy's ask-not-what-your-country-can-do-for-you statement (in his 1961 Inaugural Address) represents a unique

rhetorical structure. To include the sentence in an oral or written report, replacing country with company or industry or organization, would be plagiarism. In addition, the writer defining plagiarism today would likely list audiovisuals, such as charts, infographics, maps, photographs, podcasts, slide decks, videos, and webinars.

Not all cultures view plagiarism as inappropriate behavior. In fact, in a collectivist culture, such as those of China, Japan, and Korea—where the needs of a group or a community are valued over those of an individual—the concept of intellectual property seems illogical. In collectivist settings, people learn early, in the name of scholarship, to synthesize the ideas of many different authors and their own with no acknowledgment of sources. Conversely, individualistic societies, like the United States, Great Britain, and Australia—where high value is placed on individual achievement—accept the notion of nonmaterial property or individual ownership of ideas and, in turn, equate plagiarism with theft.

Avoiding Plagiarism in Written Reports

Clearly, the leading way to avoid plagiarizing in a report is to be conscientious about acknowledging the secondary sources used in it. Subsequent sections of this chapter will help you do that. Organizing your materials and continually improving your documentation skills will guard against accidental plagiarism. And knowing what plagiarism is and its consequences in your setting also helps you prevent it. Following these guides will help you avoid plagiarism.

- Manage time and organize materials. Plan your reports carefully and start early. Generally, when you rush to meet a deadline, even a self-imposed one, you are more likely to make careless mistakes and to take foolish risks just to get done.[3]
  - Find reference information for a book on the *copyright page*, near the front cover with "Copyright" or the © symbol or both displayed.
  - For a periodical reference, look for a page showing the date, *volume number*, and issue number near the beginning of the periodical.

- ○ To reference a web page, record the page title (top), publication date (top or bottom) or last-modified date (bottom or top), and the *universal resource locator*, or URL (address box) or the *digital object identifier*, or DOI (where to find it). In addition, record the article title and author's name (if any).
- ○ Consider using two font or ink colors for writing notes, say, black for paraphrased notes and blue for verbatim notes (quotations).[4]
- Do not overlook the obvious. No matter where you find it, give credit for words, information, and ideas that you learn during your research—even if it comes from your own daily newspaper or *Wikipedia* or a blog you follow regularly.[5]
- When forming a project team, collaborate on writing procedures and policies for the team to follow. Include specific procedures for avoiding plagiarism and spell out how the team will deal with plagiarism and the plagiarizer if it occurs.
- Enhance your citing skills. Know what documentation styles are available to you. Perhaps your organization prescribes a style for all reports. If you are submitting a report for publication, the publisher will likely dictate the documentation style. In academic settings, instructors often indicate a preferred or required style.

  Also, develop your ability to paraphrase properly, as demonstrated in Chapter 3. When citing multiple points from one source, cite them individually rather than giving one citation at the end of a long paragraph.[6]
- When in doubt about the need for a citation, ask a trusted colleague, instructor, or reference librarian. If no such person is available, cite the source.[7]
- In an academic setting, know the consequences at your institution for a student caught plagiarizing and do not yield to the argument that everybody does it.[8] Current technologies often allow instructors to uncover plagiarized text quickly and easily, so the chances of being caught are great, and usually penalties are high. *Note:* Students invite plagiarism when they buy reports from a website or elsewhere or pay someone to produce a report or part of one for

them. The same might be said of copying all or part of another student's report.[9] Another practice that incites plagiarism—or worse—is listing only a web address instead of a complete reference.

- Use an online plagiarism checker. Plagiarism checkers like search engines are driven by algorithms that scan text you enter, compare your text to that in the checker's databases, and identify identical or similar text.[10] If you inadvertently used the same sentence structure and similar vocabulary as a secondary source, running a plagiarism checker may alert you. Then, if you deem it necessary, you can revise your text before delivering the report to its audience.
  - As a student, use a plagiarism checker to help avoid the suspicion of plagiarism by instructors, who themselves often use plagiarism detector software.
  - As a business person, use a plagiarism checker on any report that involves secondary data, especially when you are preparing scientific journal articles, legal documents, and grant proposals. Doing so takes only a few minutes and is a worthy use of any writer's time.[11] Whenever you delegate secondary data collection to a freelance writer or intern, remember to run a checker on that text.
  - Dozens of free checkers—with varying performance records—are available on the Internet. The following list names commercial plagiarism detectors for your consideration.
    - iThenticate (www.ithenticate.com)
    - Plagius (www.plagius.com/s/en/home)
    - PlagScan (www.plagscan.com)
    - Scribbr (www.scribbr.com/plagiarism-check)
    - Turnitin (http://turnitin.com)

Avoiding Plagiarism in Oral Reports

When presenting an oral report, avoid plagiarism as rigorously as when you write one. Be absolutely clear about what content is yours and what is not. Naturally, you will need to adapt your techniques. The following list offers guides for avoiding plagiarism in presentations.[12]

- Always cite quotations. One way is to say the word quote before giving the quotation and the word unquote after giving it. If this technique seems overformal, or if your talk includes many quotations, use the same wording you would use to write the quotation.
  - Example: On the TopRank blog in 2014, Nicolette Beard wrote the following statements about using print newsletters for direct marketing. Then give the quotation.
  - If the quotation runs more than two or three short sentences, say still quoting before continuing.
  - Clearly indicate where the quotation ends.
- Cite paraphrased content, too. Instead of noting precisely where the cited material begins and ends, blend your attribution with the flow of ideas in the paraphrase. Example: In his 2013 CompanyNewsletters blog, David Kandler recommended scheduling seven hours to create each 8.5x11 newsletter page, plus time for designing, proofing, and correcting.
- You may not need to cite certain literary mechanisms—such as adages, clichés, one-liners, and proverbs—sayings that are compelling because the audience is aware of their origin.
  - If analysis of your audience suggests they may be unfamiliar with the stylistic device in question, cite its source or at least note that you did not originate the saying. Since most such devices are deeply rooted in the speaker's culture, be careful when speaking to a culturally diverse audience.
  - Cite an anonymous saying this way: It has often been said, "A little knowledge is a dangerous thing."
  - When the originator of a saying is known, cite it like this: As Ben Franklin reminds us, "A penny saved is a penny earned."
  - You do not need to cite the source of slides downloaded from your organization's slide library. Supposedly, those slides were preapproved for use; and any necessary references are already in place.
  - If your slide deck includes someone else's work or ideas, regardless of the form—audio clip, graph, map, photo, text, video—cite the source. (Some photos may not require a citation, as noted on

page 132.) Place a short reference, like the in-text references in Chapter 3, on the slide to which it pertains. Then list all complete references on one slide (more if absolutely necessary) at the end of the deck. See Figure 4.1(a) and (b).

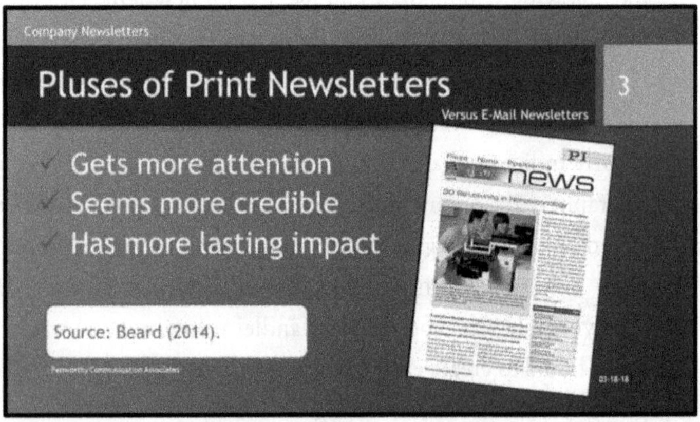

Figure 4.1(a) Source citation on a content slide

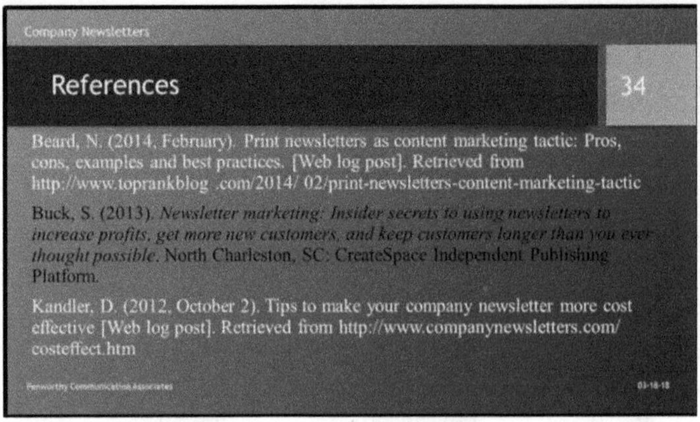

Figure 4.1(b) References list in a slide deck

Plagiarism is among the most serious and most common ethical problems in academia and business.[13] Following the preceding guides will help you avert plagiarism in your written and oral reports.

Copyright Infringement: Similar but Not the Same

Simply documenting sources and checking for plagiarism do not guard against *copyright infringement*, which involves reproducing copyrighted work without obtaining permission from the individual or company that owns the copyright.[14] Creative works are covered by some form of *intellectual property law*. Intellectual property involves expressions, ideas, and names that are protected from misuse by copyrights, patents, and trademarks, respectively. Laws protecting intellectual property have one overriding purpose: to encourage creative expression. This encouragement comes in the U.S. Copyright Law in the form of exclusive rights for authors and artists to create and sell their works, to create derivative works, and to display or perform their works in public.[15]

Copyright law secures ownership of audio, print, and visual expressions as soon as they are made tangible. Copyright protection is commonly represented with this symbol: ©. For example, an e-book, DVD, journal article, or web page is copyrighted the moment it exists, with or without a formal notice, or ©.[16] Copyright law applies to products of the visual and performing arts; in addition, it applies to books, blogs, corporate reports, data displays (charts, graphs, tables), photographs, podcasts, slide templates, and software packages.[17] *Note:* Materials published by the U.S. Government are notable exceptions. For example, you may use data provided by the U.S. Census Bureau in your business reports without worry of copyright infringement.[18]

While plagiarism is an ethical breakdown, copyright infringement is a violation of federal law. As such, copyright infringement consequences include civil and—increasingly—criminal penalties.[19] *Notes:* A person liable for civil copyright infringement may be court-ordered to pay damages of $750 to $30,000 to the copyright holder, or owner, for each infringed work. If the court finds infringement to be intentional, it may award up to $150,000 for each infringed work, plus costs and attorneys' fees. Furthermore, deliberate copyright infringement can also result in criminal penalties, including up to 5 years' imprisonment and fines up to $250,000 per offense.[20] (For details, see Copyright Law of the United States, Title 17, Sections 504, 505.[21])

Two kinds of material are exempt from copyright law: common knowledge and material in the public domain. *Common knowledge* "is knowledge that is known by everyone or nearly everyone, usually with reference to the community in which the term is used."[22] *Public domain* refers to material that anyone can use and share without seeking permission, paying a fee, or even citing its source. Material enters the public domain if not copyrighted at its inception (exceedingly rare as already explained), if the copyright has expired (generally 70 years after the year of the author's death), or if the copyright is forfeited by the person or entity that owns it. As noted earlier, U.S. Government publications are considered to be in the public domain from their inception.

Generally, works published in the U.S. before 1923 are also exempt from copyright law. Likewise, copyright law does not apply to simple (unembellished) concepts, discoveries, ideas, principles, or procedures.[23]

Some creators—especially photographers—wish to share their works either for free or for proper attribution; and these terms of use are usually in the form of a license.[24] Before downloading a photograph from the web, look for one of these license labels: CC0 or CCZ. The initials stand for Creative Commons. The CC0 label indicates photos that are free initially and royalty-free as you continue to use them. A CCZ photo can be downloaded and used any way you want, for commercial or noncommercial purposes, without charge and without your requesting permission. Some free photos are labeled Creative Commons with attribution. This license is like CC0—but with the condition that you include a photo credit. The credit usually involves the photographer's name and a link to his or her website, but check for and use the photo credit specified.[25] Credits may be placed under each photo or in an appended list.

If both the CC0 and CCZ labels are missing, assume the image is copyrighted. In that case, contact the site where you found the image or contact the copyright holder directly. If you do not know the original source, do a reverse search using Google Images (https:images.google.com). Blogger Lee Geremoth explains how: Save the image to your desktop. Then go to the Google Images website. From your desktop, drag and drop the photo into the Google Images search field. Websites on the displayed list likely contain the image.[26]

Another copyright exemption so to say is based on the doctrine of fair use.

Copyrights and Fair Use

The heart of copyright law is the *fair-use doctrine*. This legal doctrine offsets the restrictions of copyright law so that it, in keeping with the First Amendment, does not constrict society's freedom of expression unduly.[27] The fair-use doctrine furnishes a context for courts to determine whether use is fair. The doctrine also indicates uses that may qualify as fair; namely, commentary, criticism, and news reporting as well as teaching, scholarship, and research. Fair use concentrates on four usage factors.[28]

- *Purpose and character of use.* In general, courts are inclined to approve noncommercial and nonprofit educational uses as fair. However, this statement is not ironclad. For instance, uses made by a nonprofit educational institution may be deemed commercial if they are profit-making, and therefore not subject to fair use.[29] Courts will balance purpose and character of use with the other three factors. *Note:* Uses that add something new, bringing further purpose or different character to the work, are more likely to be counted fair. Such adaptation of an original work is called transformative use; also, a derivative work.
- *Nature of the copyrighted material.* Generally, using a fanciful work that can be expressed in many different ways—such as a film, novel, or piece of music—is less likely to be considered fair use than would use of a factual work that can be expressed in limited ways—such as this book or a magazine or newsletter article. That is, the more imagination that goes into a work the more heavily that work is copyright-protected. Visual works, especially those involving high resolution, full color are highly protected by

the copyright law. Also, use of an unpublished work, such as a Master's thesis, is less likely to be considered fair than use of a published work.

- *Proportion or extent of the work used.* In general, after courts study the quantity and quality of the used material, use of a large portion is less likely to be considered fair than use of a small portion. However, exceptions abound.

- *Effect of use on current and future marketability of the copyrighted work.* Courts consider not only whether use of the copyrighted material will displace sales of the original work but also whether the copyright owner will be substantially harmed if current conditions become widespread.

On his website CopyLaw, Jassin referred to fair use as a balancing act. The doctrine, he noted, is designed to balance society's ideal of free speech with the property rights of individual artists and authors. Jassin emphasized that the fair use doctrine serves as a defense to copyright infringement and should never be viewed as one's right under Federal law.[30] For additional detail about the fair use doctrine and guidelines for following it, see Copyright Law of the United States, Title 17, Section 107.[31] For a concise overview of copyright law from the fundamental concepts discussed here to provisions of the Digital Millennium Copyright Act, see *Copyright Law in a Nutshell* by LaFrance.[32]

We began this discussion by defining copyright infringement as reproducing copyrighted material without permission from the copyright holder or owner. Therefore, you may assume that obtaining said permission is the primary means of avoiding copyright infringement. The following guides elaborate on that point.

Avoiding Copyright Infringement in Written and Oral Reports

When a copyright owner sues an infringer in Federal court, that legal action can be discomfiting, costly, and criminal.[33] As a creator of written and oral business reports, you may be at risk; so, know copyright law and stay up to date on changes to it. The following guides may prove helpful.

- Assume that any intellectual property you find on the Internet or on paper is copyrighted. The presence of © will confirm that fact, but absence of the symbol does not indicate public domain.
- When quoting from a source, use only as much text as necessary to make your point. Also, when paraphrasing a source, summarize concisely in your words rather than giving a superficial paraphrase. Include a citation and reference for every quotation and paraphrase.
- When using significant portions of the work of another, ask the copyright owner in writing for permission to use the work. Send a business letter or e-mail to the organization's Legal Department (or other, more precise, designation if known). (APA's Copyright Permission Request Form—www.apa.org/about/ contact /copyright/seek-permission.aspx—serves as a guide for requesting permission from other publishers and is available in PDF and Microsoft Word formats.)[34] Specify what you want to use, where and how you will use it, and the length of time the material will be in use. Also, include a replica of the material in use, showing any adaptations, you will introduce to the work and how the copyright holder will be acknowledged. Following this procedure, this book's author requested permission to use the CompanyNewsletters.com website featured in Figure 3.6.
- Know the differences between copyrights, patents, and trademarks. All of them are means of protecting intellectual property; otherwise, the three have almost nothing in common. So, if you are knowledgeable about patents or trademarks, you should not assume that knowledge applies to copyrights.[35]
- Recognize fair use as a complex doctrine. Experience has shown that nonlawyers are largely incapable of predicting the outcome of fair use cases. Therefore, do not rely on fair use claims to exonerate you should you infringe.[36]
- When you download a photo to use in a slide deck, form the habit of citing the source, even if the creative commons license does not require it. However, if you will put up your slides for wide

distribution—on Speaker Deck (speakerdeck.com), for example—ask the copyright owner for permission to use the photo in addition to citing it. Also, ask permission if your slide deck is designed to generate income for you or your organization. Example: a slide deck for presenting a proposal that, if accepted, will result eventually in a profit for the company you represent.[37]

- Take absolutely no risks with copyrights owned by Disney, Lionsgate, Time Warner, Vivendi, and Walmart. These organizations enforce copyrights aggressively and pursue infringement charges relentlessly.[38]
- If you ever receive a cease-and-desist letter or e-mail from a copyright owner, stop using the work immediately, whatever that entails; offer a sincere apology; and hope the lapse will be excused.[39]

As a report writer and presenter, become thoroughly familiar with U.S. copyright law and keep up with changes. Additional information is available at Copyright.gov (www.copyright.gov) and BITLAW (www.bitlaw.com). If you do business globally, became conversant with copyright laws in each country involved.

General Guides for Listing Sources

A references list follows a set format. The first line of each entry aligns with the left margin (1.5 inch if the report is bound on the left; otherwise, use the one-inch default margins at the top, bottom, and both sides). All subsequent lines are indented one-half inch. This format, as noted in Chapter 3, is called hanging indentation, and the hanging indent feature in your word processing software will enable you to achieve this format either before or after typing the references.

The font name and size for references should be the same as the report body, ideally a size 10 to 12 *serif font*, such as Times New Roman, for a printed report. (For a report on the web, a size 10 to 12 *sans serif* font, such as Arial, will be easier to read.)

References are listed in alphabetical order. An individual author's last name is the most common *indexing unit*. As explained later, an occasional source may be written anonymously; in which case this guide must be adapted slightly. Use the letter-by-letter system, which is based on the idea that nothing comes before something. For example, if your references list contains an author named Hammer, B. J. and another named Hamm, J. D., which one should be listed first? Hamm, J. D.

If you opt for the convenience of reference management software (page 159), the generated list will include hanging indentations; and the sources will be listed in alphabetical order. However, you may need to change the font and font size to match the body text.

Specifying the Location of Web Sources

For sources found on the web, you must of course provide location data in your references list so readers can access your sources if desired. Since the Internet's inception, we have used uniform resource locators (URLs) for that purpose. Nearly 20 years ago, digital object identifier (DOI) names were introduced for providing location data in report references. The use of DOI names is still growing, while the use of standard web addresses (URLs) is in decline. You may wonder why such a change is necessary. The short answer is that style leaders, including APA, recommend the use of DOI names because they are more reliable over time. Therefore, to hone your report-writing skills—especially research reports—be sure you are as competent with DOI names as you are with URLs.

A digital object identifier is an alphanumeric string assigned by the International DOI Foundation (IDF), a global group of publishers, to identify a web publication. All DOI names begin with 10 and all have two parts, separated by a slash (/), as shown here: 10.1108/002517406106733332. The prefix (1108) identifies the publisher that registered the name; and the suffix, created by the publisher, identifies the object (a journal article) associated with that DOI name. (*Note:* This example, like most—but not all—DOI names, consists of numbers only.) An IDF agency named Crossref (https://www.crossref.org) maintains a registry of DOIs that have been assigned to scholarly research publications, mostly journal articles but also a few books and conference proceedings.[40] *Note:* In addition to Crossref, eight other agencies also assign DOI names and maintain registries. Crossref, the largest registration agency, is the only one named here—and in most other descriptions of DOIs.[41]

According to Crossref, DOI names should be listed in full URL form on references lists.[42] Thus a digital object identifier name and a universal resource locator will look similar, as shown in the following examples.

URL example

http://www.emeraldinsight.com/toc/md/44/6

In this URL, you see the familiar alphanumeric web map: protocol (method by which data are exchanged between browser and file server, hypertext transfer protocol in this instance); file server (host or domain and extension) on which the file resides, the publisher, Emerald Insight's, commercial server on the World Wide Web; path (toc for table of contents and md for Management Decision journal); and the specific document, or file (volume 44, issue 6).

DOI example

http://doi.org/10.1108/00251740610673332

You may see DOI names recorded various ways. The current APA style manual recommends doi: 10.1108/00251740610673332 at the end of the reference.[43] To access this object, the user would need to copy and paste the DOI name into the browser address box.

This DOI example is written in full URL form. Until recently DOI examples in this form included an additional element immediately following the protocol: http://dx.doi.org/10.1108/00251740610673332. In March 2017, Crossref asked that the now-irrelevant dx notation be dropped. Naturally, any older references that include dx will lead you to your intended source.

When web references involve a mix of digital object identifier names and universal resource locators, the URL form gives references a uniform appearance. More importantly, with DOIs in URL form, a user of a digital references list can click to access every online reference—including the data sets on which the research is based and other related, supplementary information embedded in DOI name.

The following paragraphs highlight two differences in nature and function—two advantages of DOIs over URLs.

- As noted, a universal resource locator signifies a place—a map leading from point a to point b. If point b changes (a file or object is moved), the map leads to a dead end. What Internet user has not dealt with broken or inactive URLs? A digital object identifier name identifies a document, not a place. Thus, a DOI name always refers to the same object, regardless of its location—no broken or inactive links. When a user queries Crossref's registry (clicks or enters a DOI), the registry sorts out, or resolves, the DOI, taking the user to the object's present location.[44]
- Since a digital object identifier name is assigned to an article, not to a specific version of it, one DOI name applies to a web article in multiple formats and versions. Therefore, a DOI eliminates any need for you to specify the electronic format, such as PDF. A digital object identifier name assigned to a report of preliminary findings or to a near-final draft, or preprint, of an article will be a permanent locator for them along with the official report or published article that follows.

Finding a Missing DOI

Presently, many online journal articles are not identified by a DOI name. However, when listing references, try to give your readers today and decades from now the advantage of a DOI rather than a URL by following these steps.[45]

- Check the first page of the journal article, where publishers that use DOIs usually print them.
- Query Crossref, using article title search, bibliographic metadata search, or simple text query, depending on the information available to you.
  - If you know only the title and author, go to www.crossref .org/guestquery. Scroll to the second form: Search on article title. Fill in this form; click Search.
  - If you have a complete bibliographic reference, go to www .crossref.org/ guestquery and use the first form, Bibliographic metadata search. Supply as much of the requested information as you can before starting the search.
  - If you have the text of a reference, go to www.crossref.org /SimpleTextQuery and sign up for citation matching by providing your e-mail address. Follow all prompts.
- If you still have not found the missing DOI name, try a simple web search, using the article title and the letters DOI as keywords. Alternately, try whatever online resource you used to search for articles on your topic. Yet another option: Check the references in some of your other sources, which may include the article in question and its DOI name.

Whenever you can, use a digital object identifier rather than a universal resource locator. However, when no DOI is available, use the publisher's web page address (URL).[46] Then follow one set of guidelines for using both them.

Using DOIs and URLs

Following these guides will help you deliver clear, consistent references to your readers.[47]

Include the protocol (usually http://).
- To ensure an accurate URL, copy it from the address box in your browser and paste it into your references. Likewise, if you can, copy and paste the DOI name.

- For sources lacking a DOI name in a proprietary, full-text database, omit the database name and URL. *Note:* Within an academic community where all report readers have access to the same school-provided databases, you may choose to provide the permanent URL to the source in the database along with the *accession number* (alphanumeric string assigned by the library, museum, or art gallery when cataloging the object).[48]
- When using automatic hyphenation in your word processing software, ensure that a hyphen is not inserted automatically in a long DOI or URL.
- Break DOIs and URLs at punctuation points to prevent an excessively ragged right margin on the references list.
  - Divide before a comma, dot (.), hyphen, number sign (#), percent symbol (%), question mark, slash (/), tilde (~), and underline (_).
  - Break after a colon or a double slash (//). If necessary, a URL may be divided before or after any other punctuation or symbol.
- Test DOIs and URLs in your references for each report draft. If any URL has become broken or inactive, update it if you can; drop it along with any references to it; or replace it with another comparable, accessible source.
- If you will distribute a printout of your report, remove each automatically inserted hyperlink from your final draft. Taking this step ensures that all text prints in the same color or shade.
- If you will display your report online, make sure each DOI and URL is an active link.

Guides for Listing References in APA Style

Guides and examples in this chapter follow style guides in the latest edition of APA's style manual: *Publication Manual of the American Psychological Association,* 6th ed. (2010).[49] Generally, references should contain the author name, publication date, title of the work, and publication data. Observe these guides when preparing a list of references in APA style.[50]

- *Author.* Arrange references in alphabetical order by the surname (last name) of the first author, followed by the first letter (initial) of that author's given (first) name and middle name if listed. Examples: Clippinger, D.; Sansevieri, P. C.
  - Follow the pattern for sources involving more than one author. Insert an ampersand before the last author's name. Examples: Kuiper, S., & Clippinger, D.

    Jarvinen, J., Tollinen, A., Karzaluoto, H., & Jayawardhena, C.

    If a source involves more than seven authors, list the first six authors; insert an ellipsis (. . .); then list the last author. Omit the ampersand.
  - In most Eastern countries, the normal order of a name is surname followed by given name. Therefore, you may be uncertain how to list an Eastern name, such as Liu An. When unsure, check with the author or see how the name appears in another writer's references list. Possibly the name appears as An Liu in a U.S. publication.
  - If an agency, association, or institution is the author, alphabetize by the first major word of the organization's name. For example, an article titled Infographics Guidelines was created by the Office of National Statistics, you would alphabetize the item by the word Office.
  - If no author is named, move the title to the beginning of the reference; alphabetize the reference by the first major word of the title. For instance, no author is indicated for an article titled Newsletter Design Tips; therefore, begin the item with this title and alphabetize it by the word Newsletter.
  - In a reference to an edited book, put the editor's name in the author position followed by Ed. in parentheses.
- *Publication date.* Show in parentheses the year a book was published; for periodicals, give the year and the exact date of publication in parentheses. For any work without a given publication date, write n.d. in parentheses.
- *Title.* For article and chapter titles and subtitles, capitalize only the first word and any proper nouns. Omit italics and quotation marks from article and chapter titles.
  - Give periodical titles in full, using capitals and lowercase letters. Add italics to this title.

- ○ For book, article, and report titles, capitalize just the first word of the title and subtitle (if any) and any proper nouns. Add italics to book and report titles, too.
- *Publisher data* for periodicals differs markedly from the data for books and reports.
  - ○ For periodicals, give the volume number (omit Vol.) after the title. If each issue of the periodical starts with page 1, give the issue number in parentheses. Also, list inclusive page numbers containing your cited material.
  - ○ For books (any nonperiodical publication), list the publisher's location (city and U.S. state—using the official USPS two-letter abbreviation—or city and country, both spelled out). Find this information on the book's title page. Always use the first city listed if there is more than one.
  - ○ Next, list the name of the publisher in the shortest understandable form. For example, South-Western Publishing Co. might be listed as South-Western but should not be listed as SWPCO. If the author is also the publisher, simply use the word Author in the publisher position.

If you must cite sources that are not illustrated in this chapter, refer to the manual itself. The APA website (www.apastyle.org) includes information for ordering it (hardcover, softcover, spiral bound, and Kindle). Also, many colleges and universities are licensed to incorporate all or part of this manual on their library websites. In addition, most citation management software, such as BibMe, includes rules for APA and other referencing styles. The Purdue OWL site (https://owl.english. purdue.edu/owl/ resource/560/01/) provides extensive information and examples of APA style as well as other popular referencing styles.

Occasionally you may use a source that even the style manual does not cover exactly. In those instances, combine the manual's basic guides and patterns in logical ways to help your readers find your sources if they choose. When in doubt, provide as much information as you can. More information is always better than less. Also, in the following reference examples, as well as in the manual itself, you may see abbreviations, such as *n.d.* or *n. pag.*, that are unfamiliar to you. In that case, use the standard abbreviations list shown in Figure 4.2.

Abbreviation	Stands for
c. or ca.	about (from Latin *circa*; used in contexts of time; for example, c.1900)
cf.	compare (from Latin *confer*)
chap. or chaps.	chapter or chapters (followed by numbers)
ed. or eds.	editor or editors
ed. or eds.	edition or editions
6th ed.	sixth edition
e g.	for example (from Latin *exempli gratia*)
et al.	and other people (from Latin *et alii*)
etc.	and other things (from Latin *et cetera*)
f	and the following page (for instance, pp. 5f.)
ff.	and the following pages (for instance, pp. 5ff.)
ibid.	the same reference (from Latin ***ibidem***; used, especially in footnotes, to repeat an immediately preceding source)
i.e.	that is (from Latin *id est*)
l. or ll.	line or lines continued
loc. cit	place cited (from Latin *loco citato*)
n.d.	no date (used especially concerning the details of publication)
n.n.	no name (used especially concerning the details of publication)
n.p.	no place (used especially concerning the details of publication)
n.pag	no page (used for online references lacking page numbers)
n. pub.	no publisher (used especially concerning details of publication)
no. or nos.	number or numbers
op. cit.	the work cited (from Latin *opere citato*)
p. or pp.	page or pages
para. or paras.	paragraph or paragraphs
passim	here and there (or throughout)
Pt.	Part
q.v.	which see (from Latin *quod vide*)
rev.	revised or revision
Rev. ed.	Revised edition
s.v. or s.vv.	"under the word" or "under the words" (from Latin *sub verbo*)
sec. or secs.	section or sections
sic	thus (usually placed within brackets, not parentheses, to indicate thus it is in the original document or statement)

Suppl.	Supplement
Tech. Rep.	Technical Report
trans.	translator or translated
vol. or vols.	Volume or Volumes (for instance, Vols. 2-5)

Figure 4.2 Standard abbreviations used in references

Note: Figure 4.2 shows several terms not used in APA—op. cit. and loc. cit., for instance. However, you may encounter any of these terms in the references lists you consult. Thus, this list can help you interpret those lists.

As you follow APA examples on the next few pages, note the sequence, punctuation, and capitalization shown for digital and print publications. Look for patterns; that is, ways in which all references are similar. As described in Chapter 3, keeping detailed records while collecting your data will save time when listing references and again when you must cite sources in your report.

The APA style manual addresses several types of sources, including software and archival documents and collections, which are beyond the scope of this chapter. Additional examples include data sets, music recordings, software, and TV episodes.

Listing Sources in Periodicals

As you know, periodicals include journals, magazines, newsletters, newspapers—and any other item published on a regular basis. All periodical references are similar; but, not identical.

Journal article, one author

Digital without DOI

Brown, T. (2011, May 3). More meaningful typography. A List Apart: For People Who Make Websites, 327. Retrieved from https://alistapart.com/article/more-meaningful-typography

Note: Digital journals often omit an issue number, but Issue No. 327 is displayed on this web page.

Digital with DOI

Kemsley, J. (2017, May 1). Ocean acidification reduces nitrogen fixation. Chemical & Engineering News, 95(18), 10-11. http://doi.org/10.1126/science.aa12981

Note: The number in italics after the title indicates the volume; the number in parentheses indicates the issue. The next set of numbers indicate beginning and ending pages of the article.

Print

Anders, A. (2016). Team communication platforms and emergent social collaboration practices. *International Journal of Business Communication, 53(2)*, 224-261.

Journal article, multiple authors

Digital (DOI not available)

Singhal, N., & Anil, A. (2015). Infographics: The artistic way to convey information into knowledge. *The International Journal of Science & Technoledge, 3(2)*, 100.
Note: Invert the name of each author. Use an ampersand (&) instead of the word and before the final name.

Digital (with DOI)

Thomas, K. & Bosch, B. (2005). An exploration of the impact of chronic fatigue syndrome and implications for psychological service provision. *E-Journal of Applied Psychology: Clinical Section, 1(1)*: 23-40. http://doi.org/10.7790/ejap.v1i1.6

Print

Lam, C., & Hannah, M. (2016). Flipping the audience script: An activity that integrates research and audience analysis. *Business and Professional Business Communication Quarterly, 79(1)*, 28-53.
Note: A colon separates a main title from its subtitle.

Magazine article

Digital

Hoover, B. (2013, March). Good grammar should be everyone's business. *Harvard Business Review, 91(3)*. Retrieved from http://www.hbr.org/2013/03/good-grammar-should-be-everyon
Note: To insert a URL, do it accurately and rapidly: Copy the address file in your browser and paste it onto your reference page.

Print

Hanson, M. (2017, March). Firefox vs. Chrome vs. Edge. *Maximum PC,*
   22(3), 20-23.

Newsletter article

A newsletter article may be handled as a magazine article, while an entire
newsletter may be treated as a book. Provide extra information as needed to
help identify the source. For example, the newsletter title may not contain
the company name, but this detail [in brackets] would help a reader locate
the article.

Digital, no author

The free music is out there, you just have to find it. (2017, February 15).
   [Softonic] TechAways. Retrieved from https://newsletters.softonic.
   com/techaways
Note: Newsletters may be removed from a website after 2 or 3 months. Once
an e-mail newsletter source is taken down, treat it as personal communication
(see page 153).

Print, no author

IT – Email security. (2015, Winter). *[John Good Group] Good News,* (14), 5.
Note: The number in parentheses represents the issue number; no volume
number appears on this newsletter.

Newspaper article with byline

Digital

Higgins, T. (2017, February 24). GM, tech industry at loggerheads over
   self-driving cars. *The Wall Street Journal.* Retrieved from https://
   www.wsj.com
Note: Give the home page URL if readers can search for the article on the
home page.

Print

Wilkinson, J. (2017, February 24). Goodman to retire as state fair GM.
   The State, p. A7.
Note: For newspaper articles, give the complete publication date, as shown in
parentheses. In printed newspaper entries, type p followed by a period before

the page number (or pp. it the article exceeds one page). Also, include the newspaper section in front of the page number.

Newspaper article without byline

Digital

This logistics startup seeks help delivering more clients to its platform. (2017, February 22). *The Washington Post.* Retrieved from https://www.washingtonpost.com/news/on-small-business /wp/2017/02/22/business-rx-this-logistics-startup-seeks-help-delivering-more-clients-to-its-platform/?utm_term=. b19851f027cb

Print

Lowe's joins the house party with huge 4th quarter surge. (2017, March 1). *The* (Charleston, SC) *Post and Courier,* p. B6.

Note: Though the city and state are not part of the newspaper title, having that information (always added in parentheses) may help in finding the article.

Listing Sources in Books

The following book examples may be applied to book-like items— booklets, brochures, fact sheets, flyers, handbills, leaflets, pamphlets, and prospectuses—if publisher information appears in the item. Otherwise, treat such items as unpublished or informally published works.

Entire book, one author

Digital version (e-book) of print book

Clippinger, D. (2017). *Producing written and oral business reports: Formatting, illustrating, and presenting.* New York: Business Expert Press [Adobe Digital Editions version]. Retrieved from http://www .businessexpertpress.com

Note: If a DOI has been assigned, use it. If not, give the publisher's home page URL.

Print

Schwertly, S. (2017). What's your presentation persona? Discover your unique communication style and succeed in any arena. Columbus, OH: McGraw-Hill.

Entire book, multiple authors

Digital version (e-book) of print book

DuFrene, D. D., & Lehman, C. M. (2012). *Managing virtual teams.* New York: Business Expert Press [Adobe Digital Editions version]. http:// doi 10.4128/9781606492611

Print

Booth, D., Shames, D., & Desberg, P. (2010). *Own the room*: *Business presentations that persuade, engage & get results* (pp. 167-182). New York, NY: McGraw-Hill.

Notes: Show the title exactly as it appears on the title page. In this example, the ampersand replaces the word and in the title. Insert page numbers as shown when citing only part of a book.

Book chapter

In some books, each chapter is written by a different author. Then the chapters are unified by an editor. In this situation, list a separate reference for each chapter cited in your report. These examples give you the pattern to follow.

Digital without DOI

Hinds, D. (2017). Overview—Climate change and coastal resorts and hotels. In M. Honey and S. Hogenson, Coastal Tourism, Sustainability, and Climate Change in the Caribbean, Volume 1: Beaches and Hotels [Kindle version] (n. pag.). Retrieved from http:// www.businessexpertpress.com

Digital with DOI

In the previous example, if the e-book had an assigned doi, it would appear in this format (http://doi.org/10.0000/000000000000) in place of Retrieved from and the URL.

Print

De Bin, R. (2017). Overview of topics related to model selection for regression. In E. A. Ainsbury, E. Cardis, P. Puig, J. Einbeck (Eds.), *Extended Abstracts Fall 2015: Biomedical Big Data; Statistics for Low Dose Radiation Research (Trends in Mathematics)* (pp. 77-82). Cham, Switzerland: Birkhäuser/Springer International.

Entry in a reference work

Digital (no author or editor)

Cookie. (n. d.). In Nolo's *free dictionary of law terms and legal definitions - Nolo.com*. Retrieved from http://www.nolo.com/dictionary/cookie -term.html

Note: If the edition number is given, place it in parentheses immediately after the title. Example: . . . online dictionary (12th ed.).

Print

Ferguson's. (2014). Information brokers. *In Encyclopedia of Careers and Vocational Guidance* (16th ed.): Vol. 3(833-835). New York City, NY: Ferguson Publishing.

Government report by corporate author

Digital

Executive Office of the President, President's Council of Advisors on Science and Technology. (2016). Independence, technology, and connection in older age. Retrieved from https://obamawhitehouse. archives.gov/sites/default/files/microsites/ostp/PCAST/pcast_in-dependence_tech__aging_report_final_0.pdf

Print

Defense Department, Navy. (2016). *Astronomical phenomena for the year 2019*. (House Report No. 793). Washington, DC: U.S. Government Publishing Office.

Task force report (corporate author) filed online

American Psychological Association, Task Force on the Future of Psychology as a STEM Discipline. (2010). Report of the APA Presidential

Task Force on the Future of Psychology as a STEM Discipline. Retrieved from http://www.apa.org/pubs/info/reports/stem-report.pdf

Note: The term corporate author refers to any organization that authorizes or commissions a publication, and under whose official name it is entered in the publisher's catalog.51

Listing Miscellaneous Sources

You may also obtain useful information from miscellaneous sources, such as blogs, conference proceedings, maps, and personal communication. Although such publications may seem relatively simple, they may be protected by copyright. Ethical standards also require acknowledgment of personal communications used in the preparation of your report.

Blog comment

Petar. (2016, October 25). Re: Steve Jobs on communicating your core values [Web log comment]. Retrieved from http://www.presentationzen.com/presentationzen/2016/09/shortly-after-he-returned-to-apple-in-1997-he-gave-an-internal-presentation-to-employees-from-the-town-hall-building-on-the.html#comments

Note: The commenter's screen name is used for the author name. The title of the blog post is preceded by Re, meaning in reference to.

Blog post

Fulton, S. (2017, March 1). How to bounce back after a major presentation mess-up. [Web log post]. Retrieved from https://www.ethos3.com/blog

Note: If only a screen name is available, use the screen name without inverting first and last names.

Conference paper retrieved online

Marcel, M. (2016, October). *Does frequency decrease anxiety? Accounting majors and presentations.* Paper presented at the 81st Annual International Conference of Association for Business Communication, Albuquerque, NM. Abstract retrieved from http://www.businesscommunication.org/page/2016-annual-proceedings

Conference proceedings published in book form

Bayless, M. & McKenna, C. (2016). Business communication and job retention: Developing a specific list of communication skills. In C. Wright (Ed.), *Association of Business Communication Southwestern U.S. 2016 Refereed Proceedings* (pp. 57-59).

Published doctoral dissertation or master's thesis

Rudahangarwa, I. Coffee farming impact in economic development of rural areas (master's thesis). Retrieved from OpenThesis. (http://www.openthesis.org)

Note: As the name implies, OpenThesis is an online database accessible to all web users. For a dissertation or thesis published in a proprietary database, replace the web address with the library's accession number for the document.

Unpublished doctoral dissertation or master's thesis

Clippinger, A. J. (2009). *Hepatitis B virus X protein localizes to mitochondria and regulates apoptosis in primary rat hepatocytes.* (Unpublished doctoral dissertation). Drexel University College of Medicine, Philadelphia, PA.

Map retrieved from web

U.S. Census Bureau (Cartographer). (2011). Population density by county or county equivalent, 2010 U.S. Census [Demographic map]. Retrieved from http://www2.census.gov/geo/pdfs/maps-data/maps/thematic/us_popdensity_2010map.pdf

Podcast

Mims, C. (Reporter and interviewee). (2017, February 28). The Wall Street Journal Tech Talk: Are coding boot camps a new fast-track into the workforce? [Audio podcast]. Retrieved from https://www.wsj.com

Note: Referencing Wall Street Journal's home page is appropriate since it includes a search field for entering the podcast title. If the home page did not include a search box, the reference would end as follows. Retrieved from http://www.wsj.com/podcasts/are-coding-boot-camps-a-new-fast-track-into-the-workforce/4D39DBF3-4E8D-4D0D-8777-576AED210DD1.html

Video

Heer, J. (2015). *The future of data visualization.* [Video] Available from www
.youtube.com/ watch?v=vc1bq0qlKoA

Note: Treat a DVD similarly, placing DVD in brackets after the title.

Citing Sources in Report Text

In addition to an alphabetical list of all references used, proper attribution includes citing each source in the report text. APA recommends source acknowledgments inserted in parentheses and calls this citing method *author-date notes*, also known as *in-text citations* or *parenthetical citations*. Brief in-text citations also appear in full on the references list and vice versa. Items on the references list appear as author-date citations. However, two types of in-text references are omitted from the references list.

- References to sacred texts, such as the Bhagavad Gita, Qur'an, and Bible. The standard sections of these classics do not change from one edition to the next.
- References to personal communications. Conversations (including in interviews and by phone), e-mail, letters, memos, texts, tweets, and voice mail generally do not include information that a reader can recover and verify. Therefore, omit such sources from your references list when using APA style. Do cite personal communication sources in the text of your report, as shown later in this chapter.

In-Text Citation Guides

These five guides will cover most of your reporting situations. Remember, consult the APA Style Manual[52] whenever you encounter circumstances not covered here.

- Generally, insert both the surname and year in parentheses with a comma separating them. Example: More and more organizations of various types have discovered the value of enterprise social media and are expanding use of it (Anders, 2016).
- If you include the author's name in your narrative, place only the publication year in parentheses after the name. Example: According

to Anders (2016), professional work is increasingly collaborative, social, and virtual.

- When the publication year is included in the narrative along with the name—perhaps because you want to emphasize the recency of the data—omit a parenthetical reference. Example: In his 2017 study, Anders noted growth in enterprise social media; that is, an organization's use of social media platforms such as Linked-In and Facebook to connect people internally and externally who share business activities or interests.
- If you quote a printed source directly, include the page number in the author-date note. Example: "Supporting these trends, research has noted the growing use and importance of enterprise social media (ESM) for many types of organizations" (Anders, 2016, p. 224).
- If you quote an online source directly and page numbers are missing, use paragraph numbers. If no paragraph numbers appear in the document, cite the section heading and then cite the paragraph number by counting down from the heading. Example: "The good thing about mistakes is that we learn the most from them" (Fulton, "Keep Calm and Carry On," para. 2).

In-Text Citation Examples

The report paragraphs typically may be single, multiple (1.08 or 1.15), or double spaced. If single or multiple spacing is used, paragraphs may be blocked; or the first line may be indented half an inch. The first line of double-spaced paragraphs must be indented. The following examples simulate multiple-spaced, blocked paragraphs. In most instances, this text is paraphrased or quoted from previous reference examples.

Quotation from a source by one author

In writing about collaboration practices, Anders stated: "Across diverse disciplines and industries, the way professionals get things done is increasingly social, collaborative, and virtual. Supporting these trends, research has noted the growing use and importance of enterprise social media (ESM) for many types of organizations" (Anders, 2016, p. 224).

Long quotation from a source by one author

For a quotation exceeding 40 words (use the word count feature in your word processing software), drop the quotation marks at the beginning and ending. Also, indent the entire quote one-half inch on the left. If you are indenting the first line of all paragraphs, indent the first line of the long quotation an additional half inch. Then remember to reset the original margins after typing the long quotation.

Clippinger summarized her book's coverage of print newsletter production as follows.

> Newsletters and similar documents—brochures and fact sheets, for example—remain popular for promoting businesses and not-for-profit organizations. In our digital world, print materials stand out. And many consumers, including those 18 to 34, view a paper document as more credible than e-mailed information. In addition, the impact of print materials lasts longer than that of digital materials (Clippinger, 2017, p. 77.)

The discussion includes newsletter creation methods and guidelines for content, design, and visuals.

Paraphrase of a source by more than one author

Singhal and Anil's study supported use of reports in infographics format, noting that the brain processes images faster than words. Besides, pictures inherently are more interesting than text, and scientists have confirmed that visual information is retained better and longer than textual information (Singhal & Anil, 2007).

For more than three authors, include all names in the first citation only. In subsequent citations, include only the first author's name, followed by the Latin abbreviation "et al." (see Figure 4.2). Examples: A study of business-to-business (B2B) direct marketing by Jarvinen, Tollinen, Karzaluoto, and Jayawardhena (2012) revealed that B2B firms were not fully using the digital media available. The study by Jarvinen et al. provided a line of reasoning for using digital newsletters for direct marketing.

Quotation from a group-authored source

APA's STEM Task Force drew the following conclusion: ". . . despite psychology's foundation in science and its standing as the science of human behavior, it is not fully accepted as a science by the general public. Moreover, even among professional organizations and agencies that acknowledge psychology as a science, psychology is often – too often – excluded from STEM-related funding and activities." (American Psychological, Task Force, 2010, p. 13).

Note: When the group-author's name is long, it can be truncated, as shown. The full name:

American Psychological Association, Task Force on the Future of Psychology as a STEM Discipline.

Paraphrase of a source with no identified author

Finding shippers willing to let go of outdated business practices is a marketing challenge for companies like ShipLync, a provider of high-tech services for connecting customers and carriers. Educating shippers of the cost savings and quality service that ShipLync provides is a partial solution. In addition, company leaders were advised to focus on their current tech-savvy customers, learning where to find others like them and also asking them for referrals ("This Logistics Startup Seeks Help," 2017).

Note: Not every quotation or paraphrase needs to be introduced. Sometimes the text flows better without an introduction.

Paraphrase of a personal communication source

The client assessed the survey plan as too impersonal and too scripted. She suggested introducing the phone survey in a more personal way and then using a checklist as subjects talk rather than asking them specific questions (J. P. Kingsley, personal communication, March 27, 2017).

Quick Citation Method

Some writers of business reports use an even shorter version of in-text citations. This system involves consecutively numbering entries on the alphabetized source list, as shown in Figure 4.3. *Note:* Drop the half-inch hanging indentation for the quick method; use the standard quarter-inch hanging indentation for numbered items.

References

1   Clippinger, D. (2017). *Producing written and oral business reports: Formatting, illustrating, and presenting.* New York City: Business Expert Press.

2   Duistermaat, H. (2013). How to write seductive web copy: An easy guide to picking up more customers. Liverpool, England: Enchanting Marketing Ltd.

3   Eliason, A. (2017, February 17). A mostly brief guide to writing better web content. Retrieved from https://www.seo .com/blog/a-mostly-brief-guide-to-writing-better-web-content

4   Handley, A. (2014). *Everybody writes: Your go-to guide to creating ridiculously good content.* Hoboken, NY: Wiley.

5   McCoy, J. (2016). *So you think you can write? Your definitive guide to successful online writing.* North Charleston, SC: CreateSpace Independent Publishing Platform.

6   Mizrahi, J. (2014). *Web content: A writer's guide.* New York City: Business Expert Press.

7   Sharma, V. (2015, August 27). Use web content writing for promotion on the web. Retrieved from http://robertjrgraham.com/use-web-content-writing-for-promotion-on-the-web

8   Swee, K. (2011, November 11). Writing for the web: Tips & common mistakes we make [Web log post]. Retrieved from http://hongkiat.com/blog/writing-for-the-web-common-mistakes-we-make

---

Figure 4.3 Numbered references list

Instead of an author-date citation, a source is identified by its number in the references list, followed by a colon and page number or numbers (if appropriate). The following examples cite sources listed in Figure 4.3. The paraphrase example came from Reference 8; the quotation example appears on page 7 of Reference 6.

Paraphrase example

Tips for writing web content are like the principles of all effective writing for business: Get attention and get to the point; use simple words and short sentences and paragraphs; identify yourself; and focus on readers at every step (8).

Quotation example

Mizrahi offered this editing technique: ". . . read your copy aloud and make marks next to areas that require editing. . . . If you find yourself stumbling as you read your copy, the chances are good that you have a problem . . . ." (6:7).

APA Style: More than Citing Sources

- Content and organization, naming standard and supplementary report parts and the order in which they appear
- Format, including spacing, paging, headings, fonts, and emphasis techniques.
- Illustration, describing and showing how to construct tables and figures
- Mechanics, including abbreviations, capitalization, equations, metrics, numbers, punctuation, spelling, and statistical text
- Writing style, including clarity, conciseness, and tone

Naturally, if you are writing an article for publication in an APA journal, you will try to observe all the APA rules. Otherwise, when advised to use APA style, ask whether that term applies only to managing sources or other areas of your report as well.

Reference Management Software

Reference, or citation, management software, such as BibMe and EasyBib, are also called bibliography and citation makers. As you likely know, these online programs simplify the creation of in-text citations and reference lists. Some of these websites offer a free basic version as well as a subscription plan that includes additional features. For instance, the free version of EasyBib offers only the MLA referencing style, while the subscription plan makes several typical and many unusual styles available.

In most instances, use of the software involves three steps.

1. Select the referencing style you want from two or more styles offered.
2. Choose the source type, such as book, journal, interview, or website, from the range of options.
3. Select the mode, either autocite (autofill) or manual, mode. If you choose the auto mode, then you search for your online source and the software generates a formatted reference automatically. If you choose the manual mode, you type elements of the reference into labeled fields. *Note:* In some cases—Citation Producer, Knight-Cite, and WritingHouse, for example—manual entry is the only option.[54]

To create a references list, you can copy and paste each reference as you create it into your word processing file. For added convenience, though, you can move on to your next reference; and it will be added to your references list in alphabetical order. Then after adding your last reference, you can edit the references, add a title, and simply export the entire alphabetized list into a word processing file.

In most situations, you can save your references list at the website and return to update it later. The time limit for saving may be quite short—say, three or four days—if you are using the free version. Naturally, if your references list includes many sources, you will want to be fully aware of the time limits before you begin.

Figure 4.4 compares popular reference management software in terms of the documentation styles and source types covered.

Legend	
AMA	American Medical Association - AMA *Manual of Style: A Guide for Authors and Editors*, 10th ed.55
APA	American Psychological Association – Publication Manual of the American Psychological Association, 6th ed.56
CMS	*The Chicago Manual of Style*, 16th ed.57
CSE	Council of Science Editors - *The CSE Manual for Authors, Editors, and Publishers*, 8th ed.58
MLA	Modern Language Association - *MLA Handbook*, 8th ed.59
Turabian	*Turabian's Manual for Writers of Research Papers, Theses, and Dissertations*, 8th edition.60

Citation Generator and URL	Documentation Styles and Source Types
BibMe (www.bibme.org)	APA, CMS, MLA, Turabian, and many other styles. Book, journal, video, website, and 60 more source types.
Citation Builder (www.lib.ncsu.edu /citationbuilder)	APA, CMS, CSE, and MLA styles. Book, chapter, journal, magazine, newspaper, and website sources.
Citation Machine (www.citationmachine.net)	APA, CMS, and MLA styles. Book, film, journal, magazine, newspaper, website, and many other source types.
Citation Producer (http://citationproducer .com)	APA and MLA styles. Book, journal, magazine, newspaper, and website sources.
Citefast (www.citefast.com/?s=APA)	APA, CMS, and MLA styles. Book, journal, newspaper, online video, web image, web page, and 12 more source types.
Cite This for Me (www.citethisforme .com/us/citation-generator/apa)	APA, AMA, CMS, MLA, and 11 other styles. Book, journal, website, and nine more source types
EasyBib (www.easybib.com)	APA, CMS, MLA, and many specialty documentation styles. MLA only in free version. Book, database, journal, website, video/film and 54 more source types.
KnightCite (www.calvin.edu/library /knightcite)	APA, CMS, and MLA styles. Book, film or video, journal, magazine, and newspaper sources.
WritingHouse (http://writinghouse.org)	APA, CMS, and MLA documentation styles.

Figure 4.4 Comparison of reference and citation makers

Given the availability of reference management software, why bother learning guides for references and citations? At the BibMe website, someone noted: "Even though BibMe may be very helpful in automating the process of creating and formatting citations, it's still important that [users] understand how to cite sources 'the old-fashioned way.' Knowing the rules and guidelines that each style guide outlines is an important part of writing . . .." [61] In addition, knowing the rules allows you to check the accuracy and consistency of your references lists and in-text citations and make needed corrections. With accuracy in mind, be aware of any limitations of your reference management software. For example, BibMe does not include page number references in its default mode.[62] No tool can replace your keen eye, knowledge of documentation guides, or awareness of the accuracy your readers will expect in the references list.

Summary

Writers of business reports using secondary data usually acknowledge their sources for several reasons. Acknowledging sources separates the content you borrowed from your original ideas. Also, it enables other report writers to find the data you used and build on it in their research. Your contemporaries in business and academics expect the honesty documenting sources represents. Additionally, citing sources helps prevent a lapse in ethics called plagiarism.

Specific ways to avoid plagiarism in a written report include the following.

- Plan and organize materials before you start your secondary research. Allow ample time to meet the report due date, and manage that time as you write.
- Create a reference for any precise wording, facts, and ideas that you pick up during your research.
- On a research and report-writing team, agree with other members on procedures for managing secondary data and avoiding plagiarism.
- Know what referencing styles are available to you. If possible, settle on one style, such as APA, to use for every report.

- Become adept at writing original summaries of source content. Loose paraphrasing (reproduction of an author's wording with a few words replaced by synonyms) is never appropriate.
- When in doubt about the need to cite a source, cite it.
- Know the results of plagiarism in your academic institution or profession.
- Use an online plagiarism checker, such as iThenticate or Turnitin.

Guard against plagiarism in oral reports, too. These guides may help.

- Develop techniques, such as air quotes, for citing quotations.
- Cite paraphrases by blending attribution into the flow of your words.
- If your slide deck includes someone else's work in any form, place a short reference on the pertinent slide and a list of complete references on the last slide.

Copyright infringement, the reproduction, or lifting, of an author's content into another's work without permission, violates Federal laws governing intellectual property and may result in criminal penalties. However, U.S. copyright laws do not apply to simple notions, most material published before 1923, so-called common knowledge, and material in the public domain. In deciding claims of copyright infringement, courts apply the doctrine of fair use. Fair use is determined, not by a formula, but by careful consideration of the type of copyrighted material, how that material is used, proportion of the copyrighted work reproduced, and the effect of lifting on sales of the copyrighted content.

Follow these basic guidelines to avoid copyright infringement in your written and oral business reports.

- Assume that all current intellectual property except U.S. government publications is copyrighted.
- Use quotations sparingly; quote infrequently and just enough to make your point.

- To paraphrase, summarize content in your words and style.
- Before lifting a block of copyrighted content, send a written request for permission to the copyright holder.
- If told to cease from using lifted content, do so promptly. An apology may help you avoid copyright infringement charges.

In a report containing secondary research, a references list is a must-have feature. Following the last content page, the references are listed alphabetically in a format similar to the report body, except that each entry is hanging indented. In general, each reference should include these details: author, publication date, title, and publisher. Omit any personal communications you cite. To make references precise and consistent, refer to *Publication Manual of the Americans Psychological Association*, aka the APA style manual, or another style used by writers in your field.

For references to web content, if you are not already competent at finding and using DOI names, acquire those skills, because DOIs are rapidly replacing URLs in reference lists. Stick to these guides for managing both kinds of document finder.

- In reports to be printed, remove the hyperlinks. For online reports, including PDFs, ensure that all links remain active: test them.
- If you create a references list from scratch instead of using citation management software, copy a DOI or URL from your browser's address field rather than type it into your list. Also, include the protocol.
- Prevent an overly ragged right margin by breaking DOIs and URLs before or after punctuation marks.

As you browse a style manual, note the ways that all references are the same or similar. Also notice the use of punctuation marks. To reference a source for which no example is given, simply follow the patterns in the available examples.

Citing sources in the report text is as important as including a references list. Most in-text references consist of author name(s) and publication year, but also use variations shown in the chapter.

Citation management software, such as Citefast or WritingHouse, do not eliminate the need to know basic rules of citing and referencing. However, these online programs do save considerable time and effort for a busy researcher-writer.

Glossary

Using Primary Data (Chapters 1 and 2)

active data collection. A process in which the researcher and the elements interact

analysis. The process of taking a large set of data and examining smaller pieces to develop ideas or findings about the data

area sampling. A sampling method in which an area to be sampled is subdivided into blocks that are then selected at random

bias. The degree to which a sample reflects an over- or under-representation of one or more characteristics being studied

classification. The process of categorizing data based on established criteria for deriving meaning from it

cluster. A sampling method that first divides the population into separate groups, called clusters, from which a simple random sample of clusters is selected from the population

coding. The transforming of collected data into a consistent form that can be entered into software for analysis

complex probability sampling. See *restricted probability sampling*

conclusions. Logical determinations made from the findings of the research process

convenience sample. A method of sampling which is solely based on availability of elements or participants

correlation. A measurement of the interdependence of two variables

data. Raw facts collected about an entity or situation

data analysis. The process of reviewing collected information then interpreting it and subjecting it to statistical processes

data collection. A process of gathering data systematically from various sources for solving a stated research problem

database. An organized set of raw facts about many similar entities

deduction. The process of reasoning that determines generalities with a certainty, moving from the generally known to the individual case

descriptive statistics. The set of statistics, or numbers, that describe the characteristics of a data set

editing. The process of identifying and correcting errors or inconsistencies in collected data

element. An individual entity within a population

experimentation. A process of collecting data in which an action is performed on an element to determine the response

face-to-face interview. A technique in which there is a one-to-one series of questions and answers, designed to elicit information from an element

field testing. Presenting the instrument to a group of respondents typical of those with whom it will eventually be used

findings. What can be stated, either through statistical or nonstatistical analysis and synthesis about a set of data

focus group interview. A subset of the sample, assembled and questioned by the interviewer, to generate conversation about the research topic; themes or ideas are then derived from the conversation

hasty generalization. A fallacy of inductive reasoning based on a too-limited set of evidence

induction. The process of reasoning that infers generalities without an absolute certainty, moving from individual cases to an assumed generality

inferential statistics. A set of statistics, or numbers, that suggest characteristics about individual data points, given a known value or set of characteristics about a population

in-house testing. Presenting the instrument to colleagues or other impartial critics for their evaluation

instrument testing. The process of detecting errors or weaknesses in all aspects of the instrument before it is used

interval scale. Numeric scales with a specific distance between two points, such as temperature or time; this scale does not define an absolute zero point

judgment sample. A method of sampling in which the researcher handpicks elements that conform to certain criteria

level of significance. The probability or likelihood that a statistical test result is not based on chance

logical syllogism. The process of moving from a generalization of a population to a conclusion about an individual within the population

mean. A measure of central tendency; the sum of all values divided by the number of values for a set of data; the average

measurement scale. A device used to assign numbers to an element or characteristic that is being analyzed; the type of data on the scale determines what, if any, statistical processes may be used to determine findings

measurements. The devices used to quantify data from which meaningful conclusions can be drawn

median. The mid-point value between the uppermost and lowermost values in a set of data; a measure of central tendency

mediated interview. A technique that uses some technology as the medium through which the questions and answers are delivered

mode. The value which occurs most frequently within a set of data; a central tendency measure

nominal scale. A scale of values assigned to categories of nonquantitative data, such as male or female

non-parametric. A set of statistics for use when the standard curve is not applicable to the population

non-probability sampling. A method of choosing the sample or subset of the population in which each potential sample member does not have the same likelihood of being selected

non-sequitur. A conclusion that does not logically represent the findings; Latin for "does not follow"

nonstatistical analysis. The method of making meaning from data that does not support statistics

observation. The process of gathering data about an element by watching it, rather than interacting with it

ordinal scale. Typical measures of non-numeric scales such as level of happiness or severity of pain

parametric. A set of statistics to be used when the standard curve applies to the population being studied

passive data collection. A process in which there is no interaction between the element and the researcher

population. The set of entities about which decisions are to be made through a research project

practicality. The degree to which a question or instrument provides similar answers from multiple individuals at the same time

primary data. Data generated and collected by the researcher from surveys, interviews, observations, and so on

probability sampling. A method of choosing the sample or subset of the population in which each potential sample member has the same likelihood of being selected

purposive sample. A method of sampling that adheres to some criteria

quota sample. A sampling method for gathering representative data from a group

ratio scale. Numeric scales with a specific distance between points but that also includes a zero, or bottom, value, such as height or weight

reliability. The extent to which a question or instrument provides similar answers in repeated measures

restricted probability sampling. A type of sampling that applies rules for selecting elements to be included

sample. A subset of the population from which data will be gathered to draw conclusions about the entire population

sample statistic. An individual statistic or number, such as the mean, which applies only to the sample or subset and not necessarily to the entire population

sampling error. The extent to which the sample statistic differs from the same statistic for the entire population

secondary data. Data used by a researcher, taken from existing data collections

simple random sampling. Selecting a subset of a population in which each member of that sample has an equal probability of being chosen, providing no guarantee of eliminating sampling error or bias

stability. The degree to which a question or instrument provides a consistent response over time from an individual

standard curve. A figure that depicts the expectation of how many individual data points can be found within so many standard deviations of the norm

standard deviation. A calculated measure using the square root of the variance of a set of data

stratified random. A sampling method that requires stratification or segregation of the elements, followed by a random selection of subjects from the various strata

structured interview. A process in which the interviewer or researcher follows a formal guide that provides the exact wording of instructions and questions as well as the exact sequence in which questions are to be asked

synthesis. The process of putting together small pieces of data to develop a larger meaning of the data

systematic. A sampling method that involves drawing every *n*th element in the population, starting with a randomly chosen first element

systematic variance. A difference in measurement due to a known or unknown factor

unrestricted probability sampling. see *simple random sampling*

unstructured interview. A process that uses no formalized questions or very loosely structured ones, getting the respondent to talk freely about the interview topic

valid sample. A representative sample; the subset reflects the entire population

validity. The extent to which a question or an instrument measures what the researcher intended to measure answers the intended question

variance. The measure of how far apart a set of numbers is

Using Secondary Data (Chapters 3 and 4)

accession number. Letters and numerals assigned by library or gallery personnel to each object in its collection, aiding users in retrieving the items

annotated bibliography. A list of publications related to a research problem along with a description of each listed item

annotation. A descriptive paragraph (roughly 150 words) that may accompany each entry in a bibliography

author-date notes. A means of citing secondary sources in the body of a report by inserting author surname and publication date in parentheses

bibliography. A list of published works (journal articles, blogs, books, websites, and so on) related to a research problem and purpose

commercial database. A collection of data sources developed and maintained by a commercial entity that may make it available to customers free of charge

common knowledge. Information generally known among members of the community that use that knowledge

complete-text database. A collection of electronically stored documents in which the complete text of each referenced document is available for viewing in a browser and (in many cases) for downloading and printing

copyright infringement. Replicating copyrighted work without permission from the copyright owner

copyright page. Page near a book's front cover that shows who owns the book's copyright and lists legal, printing, and publishing information

dark web. A small part of the invisible web that exists on an encrypted network and cannot be visited on conventional browsers or accessed by traditional search or meta-search engines

deep web. See *invisible web*

digital library. An electronic collection containing complete books, dissertations, journals, magazines, newspapers, and other documents

digital object identifier (DOI). A unique set of alphanumeric characters assigned to an article published electronically that provides a permanent link to its location on the web

document (v). To provide facts, proofs, or practical backing for statements made in a report

documentation styles. Formats for listing secondary data sources and for citing those sources in a report

dynamic content. World Wide Web information buried in the invisible web, not accessible to general-purpose or meta-search engines

fair-use doctrine. A possible defense to copyright infringement; allows use of parts of copyrighted works without the owner's permission

federated search. See *meta-search engine*

full-text database. See *complete-text database*

horizontal portal. A web portal designed for a diverse audience

indexable web. See *visible web*

indexing unit. The part of a name that determines its placement in alphabetical order

intellectual property law. Regulations that protect the names, ideas, and expressions in creative works from misuse

in-text citations. See *author-date notes*

invisible web. World Wide Web content that cannot be found by using general-purpose or meta-search engines

journal. Scholarly periodical reporting original research on a single topic, including a references list, and published by an academic or association press

magazine. Periodical covering multiple practical topics in one issue, with few or no references, and published by a commercial publisher

meta-search engine. A search engine that sends specified keywords to several other search engines and delivers a combined list of the search results

microfiche. Film sheets containing tiny images of journal and other periodical pages and requiring a special scanner for reading those pages

microfilm. Film rolls containing greatly reduced images of periodical literature and requiring a microfilm reader to view those images

microform. Material containing tiny reproductions of periodicals (journals, magazines, newspapers, and the like) and requiring special equipment for reading

online database. A collection of secondary data sources accessible from the Internet, including commercial, government-sponsored, and other databases

paraphrased. A method of recording secondary data by translating the source into your wording

parenthetical citations. See *author-date notes*

peer-reviewed journal. See *refereed journal*

plagiarism. A departure from truth in which a person takes credit for a work he or she did not originate, or uses another person's work without documenting properly

plagiarism checker. Online software that compares the text a user enters with content on numerous websites to detect and thereby prevent plagiarism

proprietary database. A privately owned collection of data sources that are also password protected and generally not accessible from the web

public domain. Status of a creative work that never had a copyright (or patent) or for which the copyright (or patent) has expired

refereed journal. A scholarly journal containing articles written by topic experts and reviewed before publication by several other experts in the field

sans serif font. A plain typeface, such as Arial and Calibri, without lines crossing the top and bottom of letters

search aggregator. A meta-search engine that finds, filters, and sorts results into categories, using rich site summary (RSS) technology

search engine. A type of *software* that *searches* databases for specified keywords; then, returns a list of websites containing those keywords

secondary data. Information accumulated by other authors and made available to the researcher through books, journals, magazines, websites, and other publications

serif font. A typeface, such as Cambria and Times New Roman, with fine lines crossing the bottom and top of letters, such as the lines at the bottom of *f, h, i, l, m, n, p,* and *r* in this definition

style guide. A set of standards for writing and formatting documents, ranging from academic journal articles to internal business reports

surface web. See *visible web*

tertiary data. Information found in sources—such as blogs, *World Book Encyclopedia*, many textbooks, and Everipedia—that combine material from secondary sources

universal resource locator (URL). A means of specifying location on the World Wide Web; a web address

verbatim. A method of recording secondary data word for word, exactly as written in the source

vertical portal. A web portal for a niche audience, such as a specific age group, ethnic group, industry, or market

visible web. That part of the World Wide Web content that standard search and meta-search engines can find and index

volume number. Numerals associated with a periodical (often preceded by Vol.) that indicates the number of years the periodical has been published

vortal. See *vertical portal*

web (link) directory. A catalog of the World Wide Web (all or part) that enables users to find specified data; may be human-edited

web portal. A website that uniformly compiles information from diverse sources, with each information source having a dedicated area, or portlet, for displaying information

Notes

Chapter 1

1. This discussion explains general concepts related to accuracy, precision, and sample size. For further study consult books, such as Levy and Lemeshow (2008) and Fowler (2013).
2. For further discussion of active methods of data collection, see publications by Brace (2013), Bradburn, Sudman, and Wansink (2004), and Stevens, Wrenn, Sherwood, and Ruddick (2006).
3. "Questions & Answers about Section 508" (n.d.); Henry and McGee, Eds. (n.d.)
4. Brace (2013, 37-42).

Chapter 2

1. McClave, Benson, and Sincich (2014); Anderson, Sweeney, Williams, Camm, and Cochran. (2014).
2. Dietz and Kalof (2009).
3. Naghshpour (2017).
4. Williams and Monge (2000).
5. Wagner (2017).

Chapter 3

1. Shwom and Snyder (2014, 251).
2. White and Strunk (2016).
3. American Psychological Association (2010).
4. Associated Press Stylebook and Briefing on Media Law (2016).
5. Harvard Law Review and Columbia Law Review (2015).
6. University of Chicago Press Staff, Editors (2010).
7. Modern Language Association of America (2016).
8. Boswell (2016a) and Boswell (2016b).
9. Milano (n.d.).
10. Price (2014).
11. "Portals and Vortals" (n.d.); "Vertical Industry Portal – Vortal" (n.d.).

12. Majhi (2016); "MetaSearch - Searching Several Search Engines in One Go" (n.d.).

13. "MetaSearch – Searching Several Search Engines in One Go" (n.d.).

14. "Deep-Web Business Search" (n.d.); "Deep Web: Deep Web Search Engines" (n.d.).

15. "Northern Light to Showcase its Strategic Research Portal Solutions . . ." (2016).

16. Basu (2010).

17. "4 Social Search Engines You Need to Know About" (2015); Weinberg (2015); Schmitz (2014); Moser (2014); Morrison (2015); and Cleary (2016).

18. Miessler (n.d.) and "Clearing Up Confusion" (2014).

19. Taylor (n.d.).

20. Library Guides (n.d.)

21. Bell, Derakhshani, and Bloom (n.d.).

22. Evaluating Websites (2014).

23. Shwom and Snyder (2014, 256).

24. "How to Paraphrase a Source" (2017).

25. "Why should I use a library database instead of the internet?" (n.d.)

26. "What is the Definition of Proprietary Database?" (n.d.)

27. Shwom and Snyder (2014, 257-258).

Chapter 4

1. "What is the difference between copyright infringement and plagiarism?" (2017).

2. Jameson (1993).

3. Hansen (n. d.).

4. Hansen (n. d.).

5. "Avoiding Plagiarizing: Mastering the Art of Scholarship" (2015).

6. "Avoiding Plagiarism" (n. d.).

7. Hansen (n. d.).

8. Hansen (n. d.).

9. Stolley, Brizee, and Piaz, Contributors (2014).

10. "Plagiarism Detection Software Misconceptions" (n.d.); "Plagiarism Checkers: Dispelling 5 Misunderstandings" (n.d.).

11. "Plagiarism Detection Software Misconceptions" (n.d.); "Plagiarism Checkers: Dispelling 5 Misunderstandings" (n.d.).

12. "Using Citations and Avoiding Plagiarism in Oral Presentations" (n.d.); Schwom and Snyder (2014, 423).

13. "Plagiarism Detection Software Misconceptions" (n.d.).
14. "What is the difference between copyright infringement and plagiarism?" (2017).
15. Jassin (n.d.).
16. "Chapter 5: Copyright Notice, Deposit, and Registration" (n.d.); Juetten, (2015).
17. Juetten (2015).
18. "How to Avoid Copyright Infringement" (n.d.).
19. "Copyright Infringement and Illegal File Sharing" (2016).
20. "Copyright Infringement and Illegal File Sharing" (2016).
21. "What Is Copyright?" (n.d.).
22. "Common Knowledge" (2017).
23. Jassin, (n.d.).
24. Juetten (2015).
25. Bloom (2015); "Using Images" (n.d.).
26. Germeroth (2015).
27. "More Information on Fair Use" (2017).
28. "More Information on Fair Use" (2017); Jassin (n.d.).
29. "Copyright and Fair Use" (n.d.).
30. Jassin (n.d.).
31. "Chapter 1: Subject Matter and Scope of Copyright" (n.d.).
32. LaFrance (2017).
33. Reporters Committee for Freedom of the Press (n.d.).
34. "Copyright and Permissions: How to Seek Permission Now" (n.d.).
35. "How to Avoid Copyright Infringement" (n.d.).
36. "How to Avoid Copyright Infringement" (n.d.).
37. Schwom and Snyder (2014); "How to Avoid Copyright Infringement" (n.d.).
38. Ballew (2010).
39. "More Information on Fair Use" (2017).
40. "DOI Help: Digital Object Identifiers (DOIs)" (n.d.).
41. Fenner (2014).
42. "Display Guidelines for Crossref DOIs" (n.d.).
43. American Psychological Association (2010, 198).
44. "What Is a DOI number?" (n. d.).
45. "Find a DOI for Articles" (n.d.); "Free DOI Lookup" (n.d.).
46. American Psychological Association (2010, 192).
47. American Psychological Association (2010, 189-192).
48. Sampson (2016); "Accession number (library science)" (2016).
49. American Psychological Association (2010).
50. American Psychological Association (2010, 184-187).

51. Business Dictionary (n.d.).
52. American Psychological Association (2010).
53. American Psychological Association (2010, v-viii).
54. Fenswick (2016).
55. JAMA Network, eds. (2009).
56. American Psychological Association (2010).
57. University of Chicago Press Staff (2010).
58. Council of Science Editors (2014).
59. Modern Language Association of America (2016).
60. Turabian and Booth (2013).
61. "Citation Guides" (n.d.).
62. "Citation Guides" (n.d.).

References

"4 Social Search Engines You Need to Know About." 2015. *Ingenex Digital Marketing.* http://ingenexdigital.com/4-social-search-engines-need-know

"Accession number (library science)." 2016. Wikipedia. https://en.wikipedia.org /wiki/Accession_number_(library_science)

American Psychological Association. 2010. *Publication Manual of the American Psychological Association,* 6th ed. Washington, DC: American Psychological Association.

Anderson, D. R., D. J. Sweeney, T. A. Williams, J. D. Camm, and J. J. Cochran. 2014. *Statistics for Business and Economics.* 12th ed. Mason, OH: South-Western, Cengage Learning.

The Associated Press. 2016. *The Associated Press Stylebook 2016 and Briefing on Media Law.* New York: The Associated Press.

"Avoiding Plagiarism." n.d. The Writing Place. Northwestern University. www .writing.northwestern.edu/avoiding-plagiarism (accessed February 13, 2017).

"Avoiding Plagiarism: Mastering the Art of Scholarship." 2015. University of California, Davis. http://sja.ucdavis.edu/files/plagiarism.pdf

Ballew, J. 2010. "How to Avoid Copyright Violations." *Bright Hub.* www .brighthub.com/office/entrepreneurs/articles/38680.aspx

Basu, S. 2010. "10 Search Engines to Explore the Invisible Web." *MUO* (Make Use of). www.makeuseof.com/tag/10-search-engines-explore-deep-invisible-web

Bell, C., D. Derakhshani, and E. Bloom. n.d. "Consumer Reports WebWatch Guidelines." *Consumer Union.* www.consumersunion.org/news/consumer-reports-webwatch-gu

Bloom, H. 2015. "15 Places to Find Free Stock Images Without Watermarks." *Harry Vs. Internet.* www.harryvsinternet.com/15-places-find-free-stock-images-without-watermarksidelines (accessed December 7, 2016).

Boswell, W. 2016a. "The Top Ten Web Search Tricks Everyone Should Know." *Lifewire.* www.lifewire.com/web-search-tricks-to-know-4046148

Boswell, W. 2016b. "What Does Boolean Search Really Mean?" *Lifewire.* www .lifewire.com/what-does-boolean-search-3481475

Brace, I. 2013. *Questionnaire Design.* 3rd ed. London and Philadelphia: Kogan Page.

Bradburn, N., S. Sudman, and B. Wansink. 2004. *Asking Questions.* San Francisco: Jossey-Bass.

Business Dictionary. n.d. www.businessdictionary.com/definition/ corporate-author.html (accessed April 29, 2017).

"Chapter 1: Subject Matter and Scope of Copyright." n.d. Copyright.gov. www .copyright.gov/title17/92chap1.html (accessed May13, 2017).

"Chapter 5: Copyright Notice, Deposit, and Registration." (n.d.). Copyright.gov. www.copyright.gov/title17/92chap5.html#504 (accessed May 13, 2017).

"Citation Guides." n.d. BibMe. www.bibme.org/citation-guide (accessed April 3, 2017).

"Clearing Up Confusion: Deep Web vs. Dark Web." 2014. BrightPlanet. https:// brightplanet.com/ 2014/03/clearing-confusion-deep-web-vs-dark-web

Cleary, I. (2016). "5 Great Tools for Social Media Search." *RazorSocial.* www .razorsocial.com/4-great-tools-for-searching-social-media

"Common Knowledge." 2017. Wikipedia, The Free Encyclopedia. http:// en.wikipedia.org/wiki/Common_knowledge

"Copyright and Fair Use." n.d. Harvard University Office of the General Counsel. https://ogc .harvard.edu/pages/copyright-and-fair-use (accessed May 29, 2017).

"Copyright and Permissions: How to Seek Permission Now." n.d. American Psychological Association. www.apa.org/about/ contact/copyright/seek-permission.aspx (accessed May 29, 2017).

"Copyright Infringement and Illegal File Sharing." (2016). Villanova University UNIT. www.1.villanova.edu/villanova/unit/policies/Acceptable Use/copyright.html

Council of Science Editors. 2014. *The CSE Manual for Authors, Editors, and Publishers*, 8th ed. Chicago: University of Chicago Press.

"Deep-Web Business Search." n.d. The TMC Library. library.tmc.edu/database /biznar-deep-web-business-search (accessed December 14, 2016).

"Deep Web: Deep Web Search Engines." n.d. MSU Billings Library. libguides. msubillings.edu/c.php?g=242182&p=1610149 (accessed December 15, 2016).

Dietz, T., and L. Kalof. 2009. *Introduction to Social Statistics.* Hoboken: Wiley-Blackwell.

"Display Guidelines for Crossref DOIs—effective March 2017." n.d. Crossref DOI display. https://www.crossref.org/display-guidelines (accessed April 5, 2017).

"DOI Help: Digital Object Identifiers (DOIs)." n.d. Walden University. http:// academicguides .waldenu.edu/doi (accessed April 12, 2017).

"Evaluating Websites: A Checklist." 2014. University of Maryland Libraries. www.lib.umd.edu/binaries/content/assets/public/usereducation/evaluating-web-sites-checklist-form.pdf

Fenner, M. 2014. "What is a DOI?" http://blog.martinfenner.org/2014/08/06 /2hat-is-doi

Fenswick, I. 2016. 25 "Best Free Online Citation Generators." SmartStudy. http://smart.study/ blog/25-best-free-online-citation-generators

"Find a DOI for Articles." n.d. Baylor University. www.baylor.edu/li9b/electrres /index.php?id =49231 (accessed April 5, 2017).

Fowler, F. J. 2013. *Survey Research Methods*, 5th ed. Thousand Oaks, CA: Sage Publications.

"Free DOI Lookup." n.d. Crossref. https://www.crossref.org/guestquery (accessed April 5, 2017).

Germeroth, L. 2015. "Proper Image Use: How to Avoid Copyright Infringement on the Web." Paragon Digital Marketing. https://paragondigital.com/blog /how-to-avoid-copyright-infringement

Hansen, K. n.d. "10 Tips for Avoiding Plagiarism." My College Success Story. www.mycollegesuccessstory.com/academic-success-tools/avoiding-plagiarism.html (accessed May 10, 2017).

Harvard Law Review and Columbia Law Review. 2015. *The Bluebook: A Uniform System of Citation*. 20th ed. Cambridge, MA: Harvard Law Review Association.

Henry, S. L. and L. McGee, Editors. n.d. "Accessibility." World Wide Web Consortium (W3C). www.w3.org/standards/webdesign/accessibility (accessed June 3, 2016).

"How to Avoid Copyright Infringement." n.d. WikiHow. www.wikihow.com /Avoid-Copyright-Infringement (accessed May 26, 2017).

"How to Paraphrase a Source." 2017. The Writer's Handbook (University of Wisconsin–Madison). https://writing.wisc.edu/Handbook/QPA_araphrase 2.html

JAMA Network, eds. 2009. *AMA Manual of Style: A Guide for Authors and Editors*. Oxford: Oxford University Press.

Jameson, D. A. 1993. "The Ethics of Plagiarism: How Genre Affects Writers' Use of Source Materials." *The Association for Business Communication Bulletin*, pp. 18–28.

Jassin, L. J. n.d. "A Practical Guide to Fair Use." CopyLaw.com. www.copylaw .com/ new_articles/fairuse.html (accessed May 27, 2017).

Juetten, M. (2015). "How to Avoid Copyright Infringement." LegalZoom. www .legalzoom.com/ articles/how-to-avoid-copyright-infringement

Kuiper, S., and D. Clippinger. 2013. *Contemporary Business Reports*. 5th ed. Mason, OH: Cengage Learning.

LaFrance, M. 2017. *Copyright Law in a Nutshell*, 3rd ed. St. Paul, MN: West Academic Publishing.

Levy, P. S., and Lemeshow, S. 2008. *Sampling of Populations: Methods and Applications*, 4th ed. San Francisco: Jossey-Bass.

"Library Guides." n.d. Angelo State University Library. www.angelo.edu/services /library/ handouts/peerrev.php (accessed January 7, 2017).

Majhi, S. 2016. "List of best Meta Search Engines on the Internet." The Windows Club. www.thewindowsclub.com/meta-search-engine-list

McClave, J. T., P. G. Benson, and T. Sincich. 2014. *Statistics for Business and Economics*. 12th ed. London: Pearson Education Limited.

"MetaSearch - Searching Several Search Engines in One Go." n.d. Pandia. www .pandia.com/articles/metasearch (accessed December 13, 2016).

Miessler, D. n.d. "The Internet, the Deep Web, and the Dark Web." https:// danielmiessler.com/ study/internet-deep-dark-web/#gs.QQx2UjY (accessed December 27, 2016).

Milano, M. n.d. "Top Four Most-Used Internet Search Engines." Chron. smallbusiness.chron.com/top-four-mostused-internet-search-engines-68932.html (accessed December 13, 2016).

Modern Language Association of America, The. 2016. *MLA Handbook*, 8th ed. New York: Modern Language Association of America.

"More Information on Fair Use." 2017. Copyright.gov (U.S. Copyright Office). www.copyright .gov/fair-use/more-info.html

Morrison, K. 2015. "Cutting Through the Social Media Jargon: What are Reach, Impressions and Engagement?" Social Times. www.adweek.com/socialtimes /cutting-through-the-social-media-jargon-what-are-reach-impressions-and-engagement/626743

Moser, S. 2014. "Social Startups: SmashFuse is the New, Simplest Social Search Engine." Social Media Today. www.socialmediatoday.com/content /social-startups-smashfuse-new-simplest-social-search-engine

Naghshpour, S. 2017. *A Primer on Non-Parametric Analysis, Volume 1* (and . . . *Volume 2*). New York: Business Expert Press.

"Northern Light to Showcase its Strategic Research Portal Solutions at SLA 2016 Annual Conference in Philadelphia. 2016." Northern Light. northernlight. com/northern-light-to-showcase-its-strategic-research-portal-solutions-at-sla-2016-annual-conference-in-philadelphia

"Plagiarism Detection Software Misconceptions." n.d. iThenticate. www.ithenticate .com/ resources/papers/plagiarism-detection-software-misconceptions (accessed March 10, 2017).

"Plagiarism Checkers: Dispelling 5 Misunderstandings." n.d. WriteCheck. http:// en.writecheck .com/plagiarism-checker-tools-misunderstandings (accessed March 10, 2017).

"Portals and Vortals." n.d. Safety Business Solutions. Safetybis.com/services /portals-and-vortals (accessed December 18, 2016).

Price, C. 2014. "Escape Google with These 12 Search Engine Alternatives." Search Engine Watch, https://searchenginewatch.com/sew/how-to/2343048 /escape-google-with-these-12-search-engine-alternatives

"Properties of the Normal Distribution." n.d. Boston University Metropolitan College. www.learn.bu.edu/bbcswebdav/courses/13sprgmetcj702_ol/week03 / metcj702_W03S01T02_normal.html (accessed January 12, 2017).

"Questions & Answers about Section 508 of the Rehabilitation Act Amendments of 1998." n.d. United States Access Board. https://www.access-board.gov /guidelines-and-standards/communications-and-it/25-508-standards /720-questions-answers-about-section-508-of-the-rehabilitation-act-amend ments-of-1998 (accessed January 12, 2017).

Reporters Committee for Freedom of the Press. n.d. "How to Avoid Copyright Infringement – Legal Action to Protect a Copyright. Reporters Committee for Freedom of the Press." www.rcfp.org/first-amendment-handbook/how-to-avoid-copyright-infringement-legal-action-protect-copyright   (accessed March 15, 2017).

Sampson, C. 2016. "Library and Learning Services." *Rasmussen College.* http:// rasmussen .libanswers.com/faq/32657

Schmitz, P. 2014. "5 Tools to Monitor Your Online Reputation." *Social Media Examiner.* www.socialmediaexaminer.com/tools-monitor-online-reputation

Shwom, B. and Snyder, L.G. 2014. *Business Communication: Polishing Your Professional Presence.* 2nd ed. Boston: Pearson.

Stevens, R. E., Wrenn, B., Sherwood, P. K. and Ruddick, M. E. 2006. *The Marketing Research Guide.* 2nd ed. London: Routledge.

Stolley, K., A. Brizee, and J. M. Paiz, Contributors. (2014). "Overview and Contradictions." Purdue Online Writing Lab (OWL). http://owl.english .purdue.edu/owl/reHandbook/QPA_paraphrase2.html

Taylor, M. n.d. "Vetting Authors of Secondary Sources. Deep Web Search – A How-To Site." Deep-web.org/how-to-research/vetting-sources/vetting-authors-of-secondary-sources (accessed December 19, 2016).

Turabian, K. L. and Booth, W. C. 2013. *Turabian's Manual for Writers of Research Papers, Theses, and Dissertations.* Chicago: University of Chicago Press.

University of Chicago Press Staff, Editors. 2010. *The Chicago Manual of Style.* 16th ed. Chicago: University of Chicago Press.

"Using Citations and Avoiding Plagiarism in Oral Presentations." (n.d.). Hamilton College. http://academics.hamilton.edu/occ/citations.pdf (accessed March 15, 2017).

"Using Images: Copyright & Fair Use." n.d. Using Images MIT Libraries. www .libguides.mit. edu/usingimages (accessed July 11, 2016).

"Vertical Industry Portal – Vortal." n.d. Webopedia. www.webopedia.com /TERM/V/vortal.html (accessed December 18, 2016).

Wagner, W. E., III. 2017. *Using IBM* SPSS* Statistics for Research Methods and Social Science Statistics.* Thousand Oaks: Sage Publications.

Weinberg, T. 2015. "6 Social Media Monitoring Tools to Track Your Brand." *Social Media Examiner.* www.socialmediaexaminer.com/6-social-media-monitoring-tools

"What Is a DOI number?" n.d. Moody Medical Library. http://guides.utmb.edu
    /DOI (accessed April 6, 2017).

"What Is Copyright?" (n.d.). Copyright Website. www.benedict.com (accessed
    May 10, 2017).

"What Is the Difference Between Copyright Infringement and Plagiarism?"
    2017. Brigham Young University: Harold B. Lee Library. https://lib.byu.edu

"What Is the Definition of Proprietary Database?" n.d. Reference. www.reference
    .com/technology/definition-proprietary-database-1a7684bedd2da89a
    (accessed January 20, 2017).

White, E. B., and W. Strunk. 2016. *The Elements of Style: The Classic Writing Style
    Guide*. North Charleston: CreateSpace Independent Publishing Platform

"Why should I use a library database instead of the internet?" n.d. Brigham Young
    University: Harold B. Lee Library. https://lib.byu.edu (accessed January 26,
    2017).

Williams, F., and P. R. Monge. 2000. *Reasoning with Statistics: How to Read
    Quantitative Research*. 5th ed. Mason, OH: Cengage Learning.

Index

OTHER TITLES IN OUR CORPORATE COMMUNICATION COLLECTION

Debbie DuFrene, Stephen F. Austin State University, *Editor*

- *Communicating to Lead and Motivate* by William C. Sharbrough
- *The Presentation Book for Senior Managers: An Essential Step by Step Guide to Structuring and Delivering Effective Speeches* by Jay Surti
- *Public Speaking Kaleidoscope* by Rakesh Godhwani
- *Managerial Communication and the Brain: Applying Neuroscience to Leadership Practices* by Dirk Remley
- *64 Surefire Strategies for Being Understood When Communicating with Co-Workers* by Walter St. John
- *Producing Written and Oral Business Reports: Formatting, Illustrating, and Presenting* by Dorinda Clippinger
- *How to Write Brilliant Business Blogs, Volume I: The Skills and Techniques You Need* by Suzan St. Maur
- *How to Write Brilliant Business Blogs, Volume II: What to Write About* by Suzan St. Maur

Announcing the Business Expert Press Digital Library

Concise e-books business students need for classroom and research

This book can also be purchased in an e-book collection by your library as

- *a one-time purchase,*
- *that is owned forever,*
- *allows for simultaneous readers,*
- *has no restrictions on printing, and*
- *can be downloaded as PDFs from within the library community.*

Our digital library collections are a great solution to beat the rising cost of textbooks. E-books can be loaded into their course management systems or onto students' e-book readers. The **Business Expert Press** digital libraries are very affordable, with no obligation to buy in future years. For more information, please visit **www.businessexpertpress.com/librarians**. To set up a trial in the United States, please email **sales@businessexpertpress.com**